PIANO • VOCAL • GUITAR

Chicken Soup for the Soul®

Piano Songbook

Songnotes by Adam Perlmutter

ISBN 978-1-4234-8549-0

HAL•LEONARD®
CORPORATION
7777 W. BLUEMOUND RD. P.O. BOX 13819 MILWAUKEE, WI 53213

Visit Hal Leonard Online at
www.halleonard.com

Romance and Relationships

Songs about romance and relationships have the potential to perfectly capture

the wide range of intense emotions one feels when in love. In this section,

we'll explore some of the greatest love songs ever written in the popular vein, from the

Elvis Presley classic, "Can't Help Falling in Love," to the Elton John favorite,

"Your Song." At the same time, we'll briefly examine the flipside — songs about

unreciprocated love and heartbreak, like the Turtles'

"Happy Together" and Stephen Bishop's "On and On."

Can't Help Falling in Love (page 9)

The lovely pop ballad "Can't Help Falling in Love" is a simplified version of a much older song, "*Plaisir d'amour*," written in 1780 by the French composer Jean Paul Égide Martini. "Can't Help Falling in Love" became immensely popular after Elvis Presley first sang it in the 1961 film *Blue Hawaii*. The tune came to occupy a special place in the singer's repertoire; he often used it as a finale in his 1960s and '70s concerts. And Presley's performances inspired many wonderful covers throughout the years, by Bob Dylan, UB40, and others. But it is the King's original version that remains one of the most enduring love songs of all time.

Take "Can't Help Falling in Love" at a gentle tempo and strive for a smooth, flowing sound throughout. Take note of a rhythm that may be unfamiliar to you — the *quarter-note triplet*, or three quarter notes in the space usually occupied by two. To feel this rhythm, you might try counting eighth note triplets on each beat: "trip-uh-let, trip-uh-let," etc. In the span of two beats, quarter notes will then fall on the first "trip," the first "let," and the second "uh." If this rhythm is giving you trouble, count and practice it extremely slowly, staying on just one note, until you feel it in your gut — and your fingers.

Can't Take My Eyes Off of You (page 12)

While pop singer Frankie Valli is best known as the lead singer of the Four Seasons, he has also done some remarkable solo work. One of Valli's most well-known songs is the brassily joyous "Can't Take My Eyes Off of You," written by Bob Crewe and Bob Gaudio and first recorded by Valli in 1967. This tune perfectly captures that rush of excitement one feels when gazing upon his or her beloved. And testament to the song's durability is the stylistically wide range of covers it has inspired, idiosyncratic interpretations by everyone from Barry Manilow to the heavy metal guitarist Bumblefoot.

"Can't Take My Eyes Off of You" is arranged here in the somewhat challenging key of E♭ major (B, E and A are flat), so be sure to take things slowly when learning the song. Always scan ahead for accidentals (sharps, flats, and naturals). Notice the form of this tune. When you get to the indication *D.S. al Coda* (*dal segno al coda*, meaning "from the sign to the coda"), find the sign at the beginning of the ninth bar. From there, take the repeat with the first and second endings, playing until you get to the indication "To Coda." Then, skip to the bar marked "Coda," and proceed with rest of the piece.

Daydream (page 16)

One of the biggest hits of the pop-rock group Lovin' Spoonful, "Daydream" was released in 1966. The song started off as a sort of compositional exercise for the group's leader, John Sebastian, who was trying to rewrite Diana Ross and the Supremes' Motown hit "Baby Love." Luckily, something completely different emerged. With its laid-back swing feel and folksy whistling, "Daydream" is appealingly quirky and wonderfully evocative of a summertime reverie. Plus, the song's old-time style influenced a number of other great tunes, most notably The Beatles' "Good Day Sunshine."

An element that makes "Daydream" particularly infectious is its use of *swing* — a rhythmic feel that's heard most commonly in jazz and blues. To "swing" the rhythm, wherever you see a pair of eighth notes, play or sing the first note longer than the second, at about a 2:1 ratio between the two notes. Strive for a playfully bouncing "long-short" rhythmic feel. The best way to learn how to swing is by listening carefully to, and imitating, other musicians, so if you're having trouble feeling the swing you might try playing along with a recording of the Lovin' Spoonful's original.

Do That to Me One More Time (page 26)

Captain & Tennille — the keyboardist/arranger "Captain" Daryl Dragon and his vocalist wife, Toni Tennille — were a late '70s pop duo that had a television show and a small number of hits. One of their most successful songs was the sexy "Do That to Me One More Time," released in 1979. This song, with its disco-era arrangement, is an excellent example of a duet between partners in both music and love. Plus, it's rather fun to sing and play.

Kicking off in the key of C major, "Do That to Me One More Time" is mostly *diatonic*, that is, the notes fall within the key. Here and there you'll see the accidentals G# and B#. These notes belong to a G#+ chord; the plus sign is short for *augmented*, like a major triad (1–3–5), only with the 5th raised a half step (1–3–#5). Note the tense sound created by this chord, and enjoy its smooth resolution to the A minor chord that immediately follows in bars 16-17. Another thing to be aware of is the song's *modulation* at the beginning of page 28. The basic progression remains the same, but moves up a step, to the key of D major, adding a bit of intensity to the proceedings.

Don't Fall in Love with a Dreamer (page 19)

Some of the most romantic love songs have been duets. Even when not sung by a pair of amorously involved singers, the best of these songs reflect an emotional bond that is particularly inspiring to couples in love. One such song, "Don't Fall in Love with a Dreamer," was recorded in 1980 by country singer-songwriters Kenny Rogers and Kim Carnes. "Don't Fall in Love" quickly became a success, hitting #4 on the pop charts. And thirty years later the song remains one of the most moving romantic duets ever recorded.

"Don't Fall in Love with a Dreamer" is arranged here in the original key, A major. The song has got some rhythms that might be a little tricky, particularly the 16th-note syncopations that occur throughout. If you find yourself experiencing rhythmic difficulty, just take things extremely slowly at first and subdivide — count, "One-ee-and-uh, two-ee-and-uh, three-ee-and-uh, four-ee-and-uh," and so on. Another thing that might be helpful is to learn the piece hands separately.

Forever in Blue Jeans (page 30)

Released in 1979, "Forever in Blue Jeans" was one of Neil Diamond's biggest hits in the late '70s. The song wasn't really about blue jeans, but rather about the simple and important things in life, such as the affections of a loved one. Predictably, though, it has been featured in a number of denim commercials, most recently for Gap®, starring the comic actor Will Ferrell impersonating Diamond. As a curious side note, Diamond himself actually sang ads for the jean brand H.I.S. in the '60s, years before he recorded "Forever in Blue Jeans."

In the key of A major, this song has plenty of 16th-note activity, so remember to subdivide if you find yourself struggling with the rhythms. Heads up, too, on the time signature changes from 4/4 to 2/4, on page 32. Another thing to note is the use of "slash" chords. When you see this type of chord, the letter to the right of the slash represents the lowest note. Slash chords are used for smooth transitions. For example, in bar 8, slash chords make for a bass line that ascends stepwise (between adjacent tones) from one chord to the next: E–F#–G–G#, leading neatly to the bass note A in the following measure.

A Groovy Kind of Love (page 38)

Around the time that "A Groovy Kind of Love" was written in the mid 1960s, the word "groovy" was heard frequently in the American vernacular. So, the young New York songwriters Carole Bayer Sager and Toni Wine put the word to use in a love song, which purportedly took only twenty minutes to write. "A Groovy Kind of Love" was recorded by the British rock group the Mindbenders in 1965 and has since been covered by a number of popular singers; Gene Pitney, Sonny & Cher, and Neil Diamond among others. But perhaps part of the reason the song remains popular is that the music is based on a movement of the *Sonatina in G Major*, by the Italian classical composer Muzio Clementi.

Starting off in the key of G major, "A Groovy Kind of Love" will be easy to learn to play — there's not a single accidental in the entire song. The left hand is particularly simple, mostly whole notes; as long as you can nail the rhythm that first appears in bar 1, you should be all set. A few other things to look out for: Just after the second ending, the piece modulates up a step, to the key of A major. Then, seven bars into the new key, the left hand bounces back and forth between the bass and treble clefs. To navigate this part, just follow the slanted lines between the staves.

Happy Together (page 42)

While most of the songs in this section are about fulfilled love, there have been some great songs about unrequited love. The Turtles' "Happy Together" is an excellent example. In the spring of 1967 this catchy song forced The Beatles' "Penny Lane" out of the #1 slot on the *Billboard* charts. The ever-popular tune has since been featured in a great number of movies and television shows, and covered by a diversity of artists, including Donny Osmond, Simple Plan, Weezer, and others.

One of the most important things to keep in mind when learning "Happy Together" is the swing feel. Another thing to note is the song's use of changing tonality for emotional effect. Things kick off in E minor, a key whose sad sound reflects the melancholy of unrequited love. But then, two bars after the second ending, the piece shifts to E major, as implied by the preponderance of E major triads. This new key, with its relatively joyful sound, suggests hopefulness.

I'll Have to Say I Love You in a Song (page 35)

"I'll Have to Say I Love You in a Song" is a great love song that was born of frustration. Purportedly, the singer-songwriter Jim Croce found himself in an argument with his wife one evening in the early 1970s. He removed himself from the disagreement, went to play some music, and in the morning presented his wife with the song. Tragically, Croce died in a September 1973 plane crash and "I'll Have to Say I Love You in a Song" was released posthumously. But Croce's memory lives on in this beautifully enduring song.

"I'll Have to Say I Love You in a Song" appears here in the bright key of A major. This is a pretty straightforward arrangement, but a number of suggestions will help make your performance expressive. First, be mindful of the different dynamic markings — *mp* (*mezzo piano*, moderately quiet) and *mf* (*mezzo forte*, moderately loud). And beginning in bar 1 of the bass clef, note the *tenuto* markings. Play each note for its full value, but articulate them so they sound separate from the surrounding notes. Also, at the beginning of bar 4 and elsewhere are 16th-note *grace notes* — play them very quickly before you hit the half note D in the bass. Simply omit the grace notes if they are difficult to play.

Just the Way You Are (page 46)

Singer-songwriter Billy Joel wrote "Just the Way You Are," a lovely song regarding unconditional love, as a birthday present for his first wife, Elizabeth Weber. He released the song on his album *The Stranger* in 1977. The marriage ended in 1982, but "Just the Way You Are" remained a favorite of Joel's fans — much to the chagrin of the singer, who has even confessed to considering what to eat for dinner while performing the song in concert. Nonetheless, some three decades after he wrote it Joel continues to play "Just the Way You Are" for delighted fans around the globe.

Included here in the key of D major, "Just the Way You Are" is written in cut time, as indicated by the ¢. Feel this meter by counting two half notes per bar, as opposed to four quarter notes per bar. One thing that separates "Just the Way You Are" from the average pop song is its sophisticated use of harmony. Chords like Gmaj7 (a G major triad, [G–B–D] with an additional third [F#] stacked on top) and Gm6 (a G minor triad [G–B♭–D] with a major sixth [E]) are more often found in jazz. Listen carefully to the different qualities of these chords and compare them to their plainer counterparts (G and G minor).

Minute by Minute (page 55)

Minute by Minute, the 1978 effort by the virtuosic American rock band the Doobie Brothers, is an album on which the bulk of the song lyrics center around love. It was the infectious title track, with the distinctively husky baritone vocals of Michael McDonald that helped catapult the Doobies to mainstream success. More than thirty years later, "Minute by Minute" is still not only one of the group's most popular numbers, but among the funkiest love songs ever recorded.

While "Minute by Minute" is written here in the key of C major, you might find it to be one of the most difficult songs in this collection. First, there's a time signature that might be new to you, 12/8 — that's 12 eighth notes per bar, 3 eighth notes per beat. When learning the song, be sure to count slowly and carefully, like this: "*One*, two, three; *two*, two, three; *three*, two, three; *four*, two, three, etc." The introduction will perhaps be the most difficult part of the song. In the first several bars, the chords change every two eighth notes, so you might want to learn the right hand separately, focusing on moving smoothly between the chords. As for the left hand, when you see an 8vb symbol, be sure to play the bracketed music an octave (the same pitch but eight tones away) lower than what is written.

On and On (page 62)

In 1977, "On and On" became a major hit for the young Californian singer-songwriter Stephen Bishop, who went on to have a small string of other pop hits in the '80s. Dealing with some of the unpleasant drama that can be associated with love (the cheating, and the heartbreaks), it was kind of an escapist song, in that the narrator finds himself letting go of all his romantic troubles in Jamaica — thus the song's laid-back island feel.

"On and On," here in the key of C major, will be fairly easy to play. To begin learning the song, make sure you can nail the bass rhythm in bar 1. With notes on the "and" of beats 2 and 4, this rhythm repeats throughout most of the tune. If the right hand presents any difficulties, just learn the melody (highest notes) before adding the chords underneath. In the last two bars of the piece are some symbols that might be unfamiliar. The indication *rit.*, short for *ritardando*, calls for you to slow down (until the end of the piece), and the *fermata* (⌢) in the final bar indicates that you hold those notes for as long as you'd like.

Top of the World (page 80)

With their refreshingly soft sound, the Carpenters — the siblings Karen and Richard Carpenter — were the best-selling pop group of the 1970s. Of all their hit songs, "Top of the World" (1972) was the biggest. This tune, supposedly written on an airplane, dealt with the highs one feels when in love. It has a kind of country-and-western vibe and has been covered by country singers, including Lynn Anderson. But testament to the song's durability, it has also been interpreted by eccentric pop musicians such as the Sugarcubes and instrumental virtuosos like the fiddler Mark O'Connor.

Play "Top of the World," in B♭ major, at a bouncily moderate tempo, in 2. Remember, this is a country number, so play the left-hand part as if you were on a string bass. (Think "Oom-pah, oom-pah, etc.) As for the right hand, when playing the chords underneath the melody, think about the percussive sound that a banjo or guitar would make. Also, when learning the song, isolate any difficult spots as needed. Bar 3, for example, contains a new chord each beat, which might be a bit of a handful at first.

We've Got Tonight (page 66)

Originally titled "We've Got Tonite," "We've Got Tonight" was a 1978 song written by the Midwestern singer-songwriter Bob Seger and performed with his Silver Bullet Band. The piano-based ballad showed a gentler side of Seger, known primarily as a serious rocker. This tune is about the seductive side of love — a man assuring his romantic interest that it behooved her to spend the night. "We've Got Tonight" was an immediate hit on the U.S. pop charts, and in 1983 the singers Kenny Rogers and Sheena Easton released their own immensely popular duet version of the song, which remains one of the greatest adult-contemporary numbers ever written.

"We've Got Tonight" is arranged here in the key of B major, which has five sharps, so take things especially slowly when learning how to play this tune. Rhythmically the song is pretty straightforward, with a quarter note triplet at the end of each phrase. Remember to look out for the *8vb* indications (play the music an octave lower than written) in bars 64-65, and don't be afraid to emphasize the *rit.* (gradually slowing) and *fermata* for a dramatic and poignant ending.

Your Song (page 74)

In 1967, several years before he became famous, Elton John wrote "Your Song" with the help of Bernie Taupin (who would become John's longtime lyricist). John was a mere seventeen years of age. In 1970, the song became his first hit shortly after he released it on his second album, which was self-titled. The heartfelt, piano-driven "Your Song" helped pave the way for the soft '70s sounds of such singer-songwriters as Carole King and James Taylor. And now, many years later, it remains one of John's most popular tunes, one he always performs in concert, not to mention one of the greatest pop songs ever written.

"Your Song," written in the key of E♭ major, is perhaps one of the most difficult songs in this collection, packed with 16th-note activity and fancy chords. So, in learning the song it might be a good idea to disassemble it and learn things layer by layer. First, work on the right hand. Practice only the melody (up-stemmed notes) until you think you've mastered it. Then, play only the right-hand accompaniment (down-stemmed notes) before combining these two parts. Next, tackle the left-hand part and make sure you can play it perfectly before combining all of the parts. If, when playing everything together you encounter a problematic spot, play each part separately again, to isolate and correct any problems.

CAN'T HELP FALLING IN LOVE

from the Paramount Picture BLUE HAWAII

Words and Music by GEORGE DAVID WEISS,
HUGO PERETTI and LUIGI CREATORE

Moderately slow

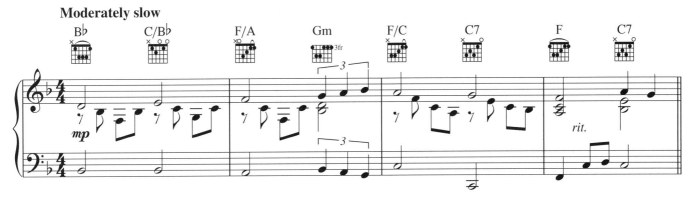

Wise   men   say   on-ly fools   rush

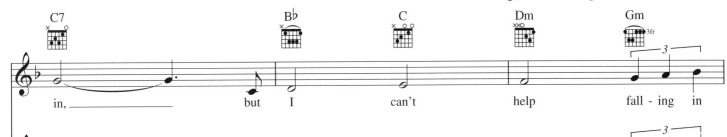

in, _____   but I   can't   help   fall - ing   in

love   with   you.   Shall   I

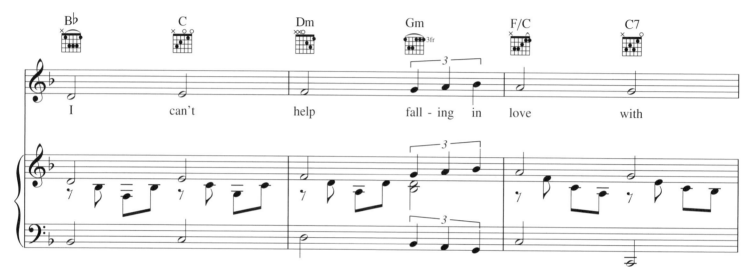

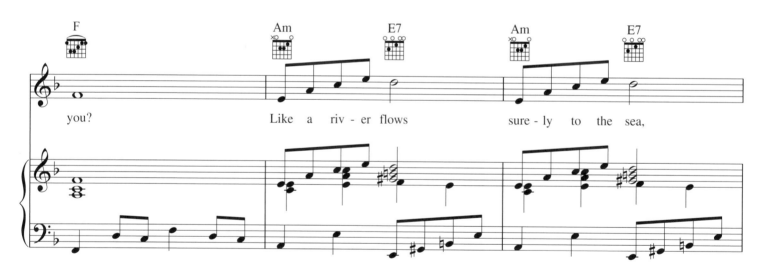

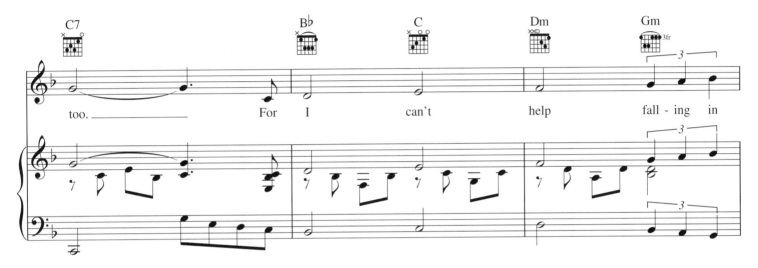

CAN'T TAKE MY EYES OFF OF YOU

Words and Music by BOB CREWE
and BOB GAUDIO

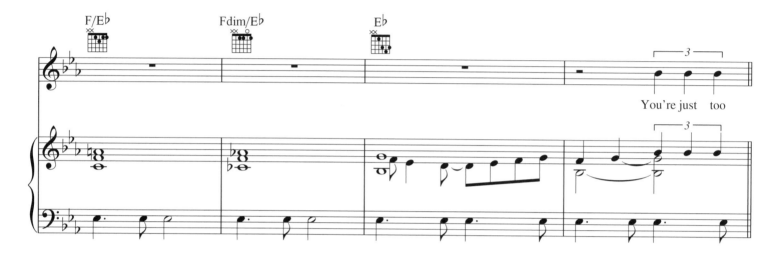

love has ar-rived, and I thank God I'm a-live. You're just too
feel like I feel, please let me know that it's real.

good to be true, can't take my eyes off of you. Par - don the

eyes off of you.

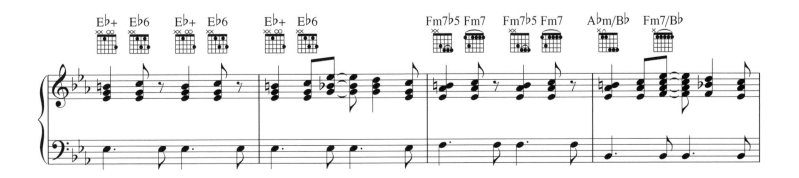

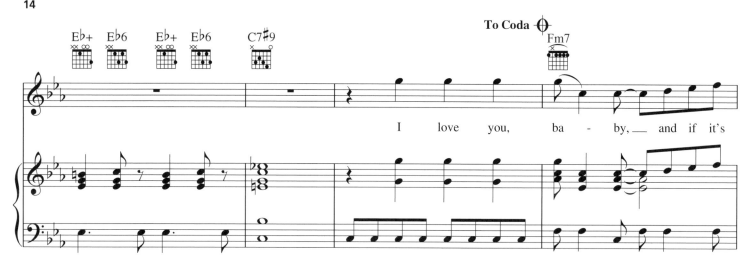

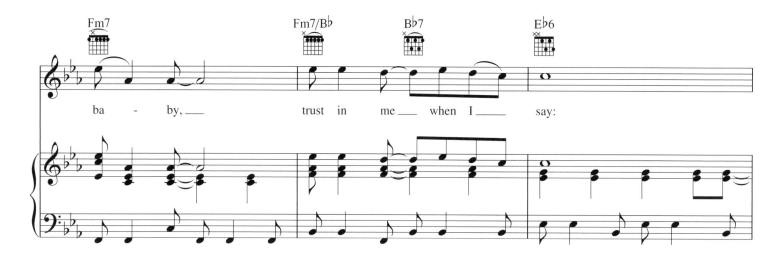

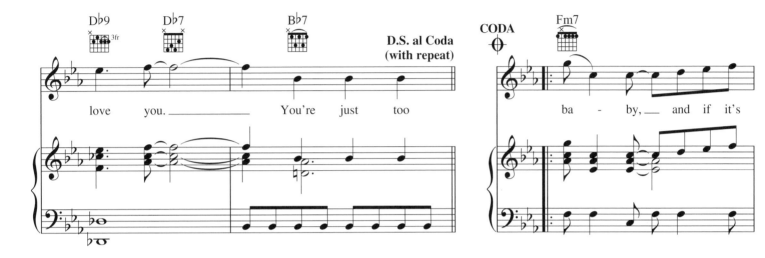

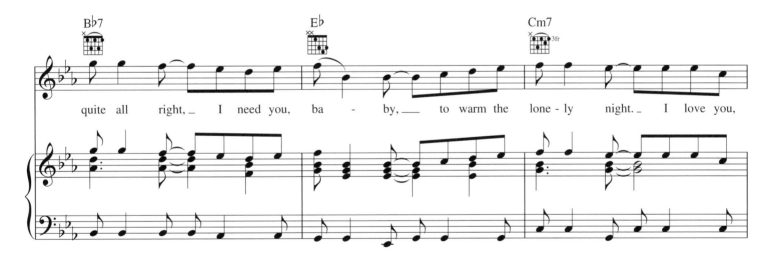

DAYDREAM

Words and Music by
JOHN SEBASTIAN

Moderately (♫ = ♪♪³)

(1.) What a day for a day - dream, _____ what a day for a
(2.) I've been hav - ing a sweet _____ dream; _____ I've been dream - ing since I
(D.S.) *Whistle*

day - dream - ing boy, _____ and I'm lost in a day - dream, _____
woke up to - day. _____ It's star - ring me and my sweet _____ dream _____

dream - ing 'bout my bun - dle of joy. _____ And e - ven if time ain't real - ly
'cause she's the one makes me feel _____ this way. _____ And e - ven if time _____ is pass - ing
And you can be sure that if you're

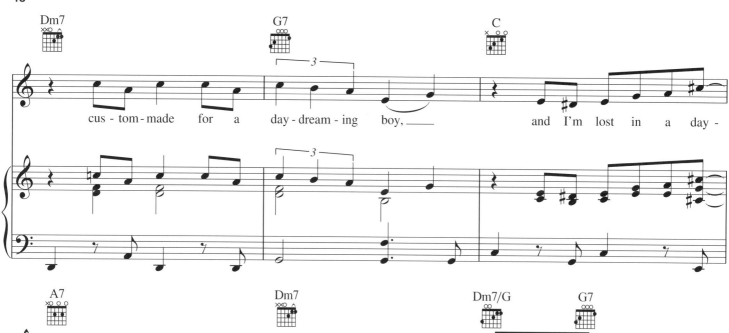

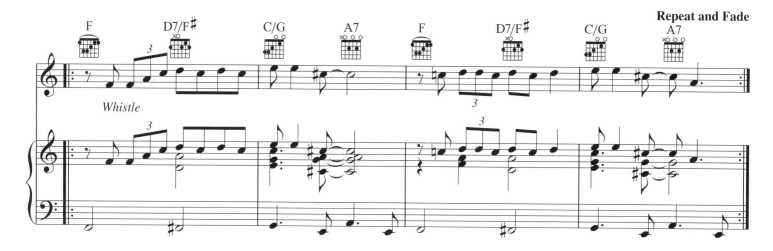

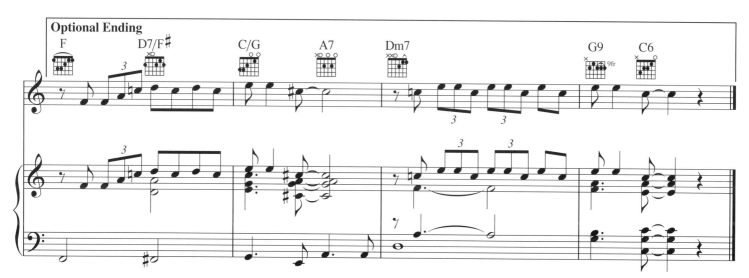

DON'T FALL IN LOVE WITH A DREAMER

Words and Music by KIM CARNES
and DAVE ELLINGSON

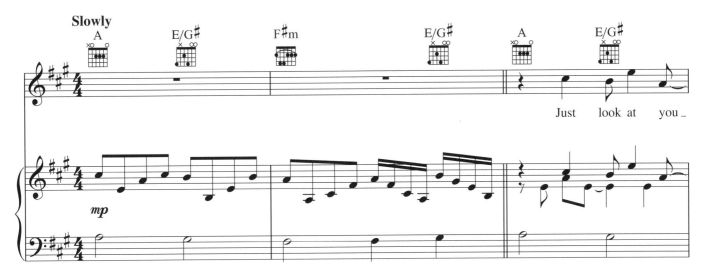

Just look at you _

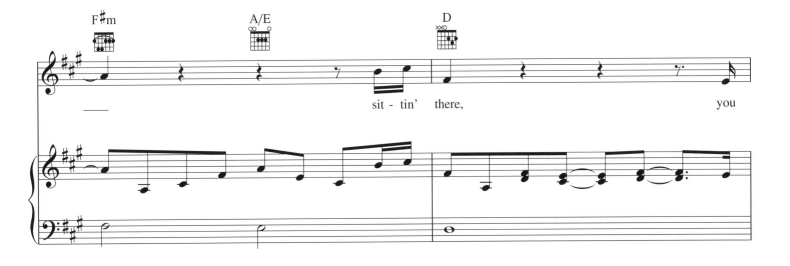

sit - tin' there,   you

nev - er looked bet - ter than to - night. _   And it - 'd be so _

eas - y to tell you I'd stay, like I've

done so man - y times.___ I was so sure_

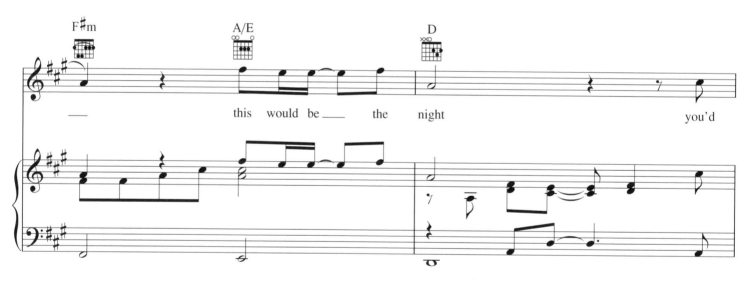

___ this would be ___ the night you'd

close the door ___ and wan - na stay ___ with me._____ And it -'d be so

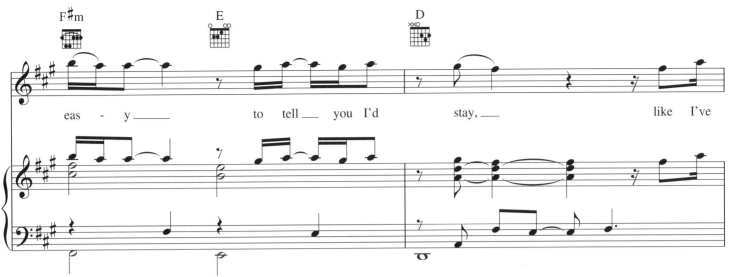

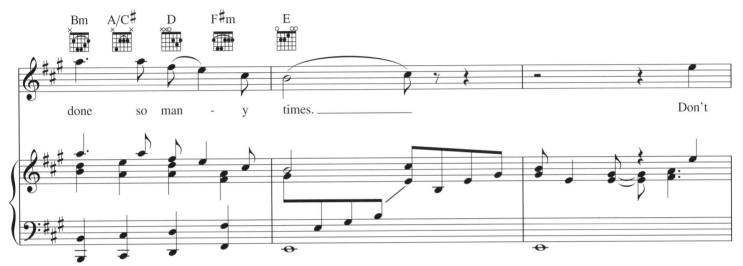

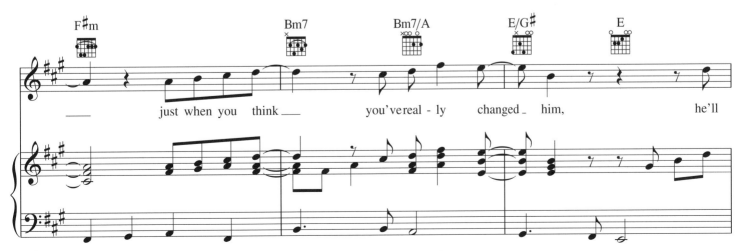

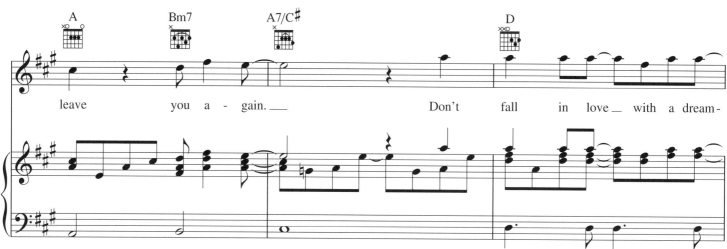

leave you a - gain. ___ Don't fall in love ___ with a dream-

- er, 'cause he'll break ___ you ev - 'ry time; ___

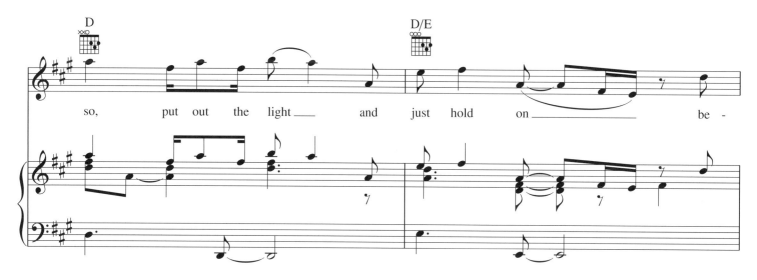

so, put out the light ___ and just hold on ___ be -

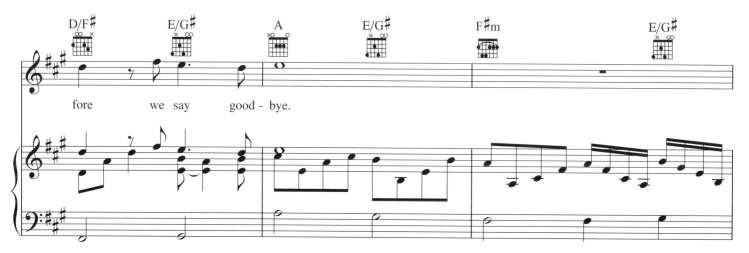

fore we say good - bye.

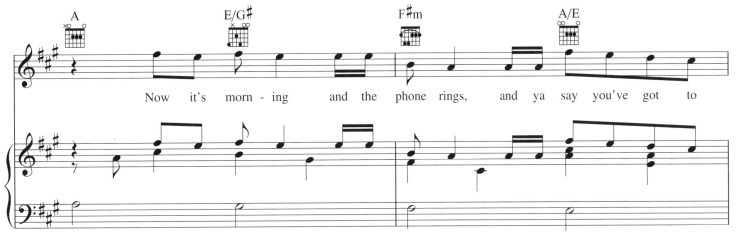

Now it's morn-ing and the phone rings, and ya say you've got to

get your things to-geth-er, you just got-ta leave _ be-fore _ you change _ your mind. _

_ And if you knew what I _____ was think-in', girl, I'd turn a-

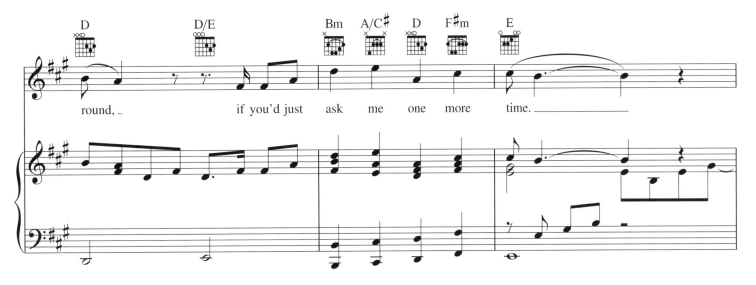

round, _ if you'd just ask me one more time. _____

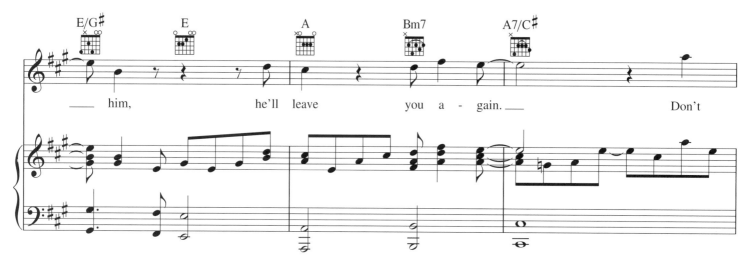

so _____ put out the light _ and just hold on _____ be-

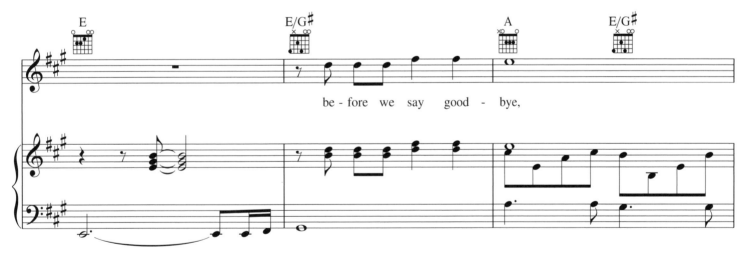

fore we say good - bye, _____

be - fore we say good - bye,

good - bye.

DO THAT TO ME ONE MORE TIME

Words and Music by
TONI TENNILLE

Moderately slow

Do that to me one more ___ time;
Pass that by me one more ___ time; ___

___ once is nev-er e-nough ___ with a man like you. _____
___ once just is-n't e-nough ___ for my heart to hear. _____

Whoa, ___

Do that to me one more _ time; ___ I can nev-er get e-nough of a man like you.__
tell it to me one more _ time; ___ I can nev-er hear e-nough while I got 'cha near.__

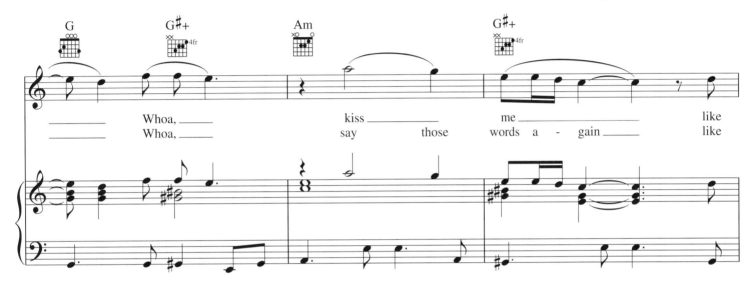

_____ Whoa, _____ kiss _____ me _____ like
_____ Whoa, _____ say those words a - gain _____ like

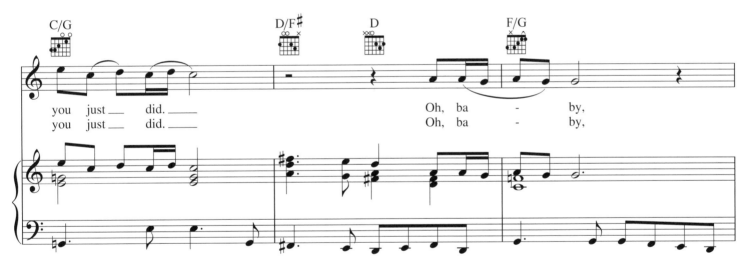

you just _ did. _____ Oh, ba - by,
you just _ did. _____ Oh, ba - by,

do that to me once a - gain. _____
tell it to me once a - gain. __

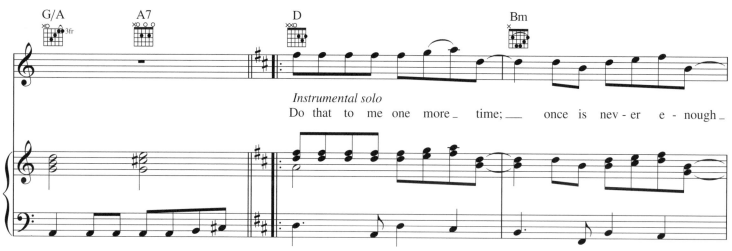

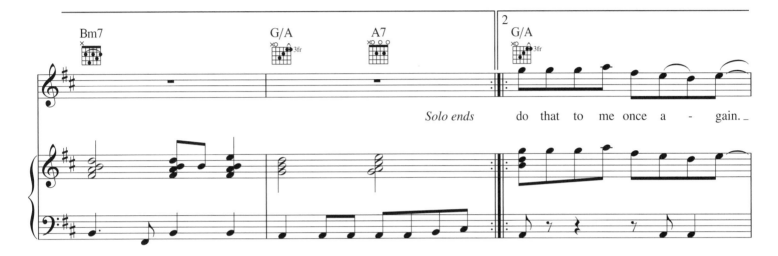

FOREVER IN BLUE JEANS

Words and Music by NEIL DIAMOND
and RICHARD BENNETT

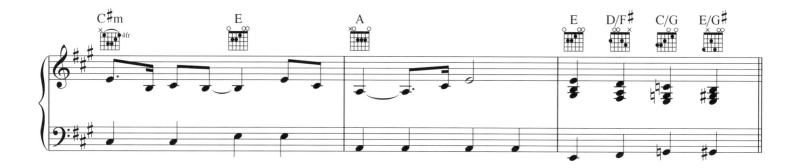

Mon - ey talks. But it don't sing and dance, and it don't walk.

And long as I ___ can have you here with me, ___ I'd much rath-er be ___ for-ev-er in

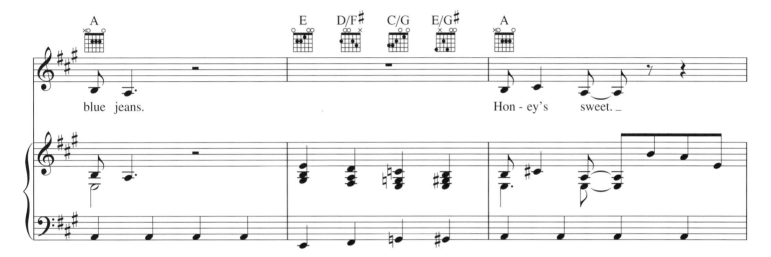

blue jeans. Hon-ey's sweet. ___

But it ain't noth-ing next to ba-by's treat. ___ And if you par-don me, ___ I'd

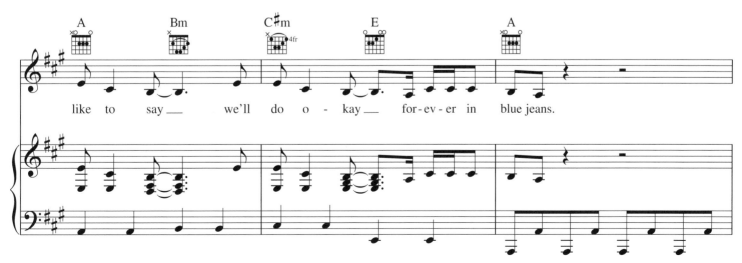

like to say ___ we'll do o-kay ___ for-ev-er in blue jeans.

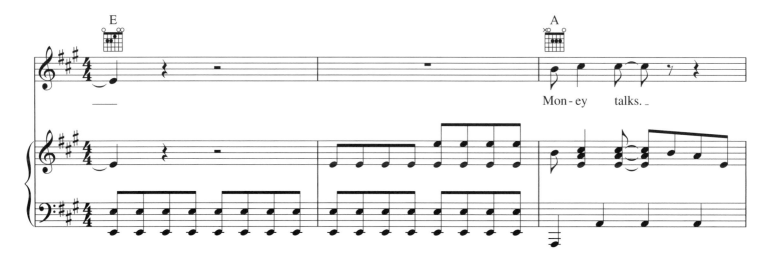

But it can't sing and dance __ and it can't walk. __ And long as I can have you

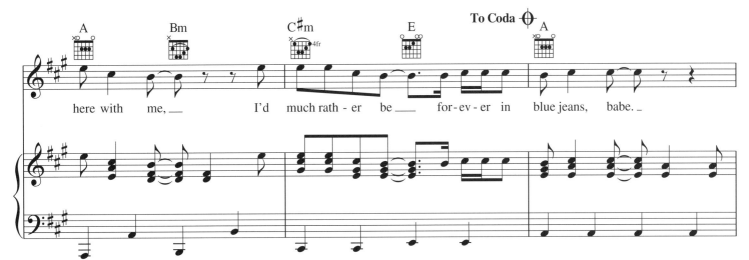

here with me, __ I'd much rath - er be __ for - ev - er in blue jeans, babe. __

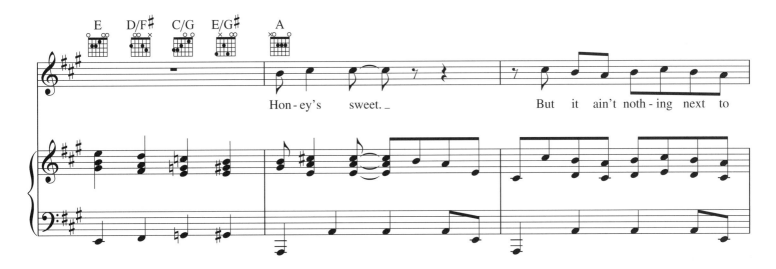

Hon - ey's sweet. __ But it ain't noth - ing next to

ba - by's treat. __ And if you par - don me, I'd like to say __ we'll

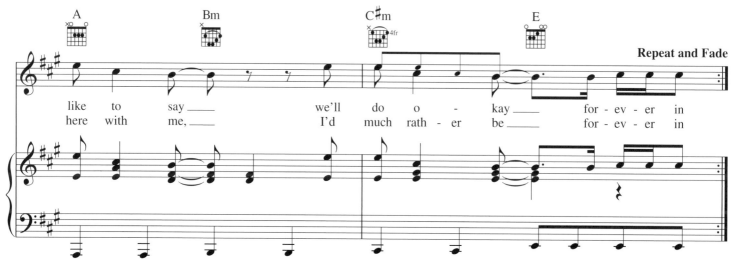

I'LL HAVE TO SAY I LOVE YOU IN A SONG

Words and Music by
JIM CROCE

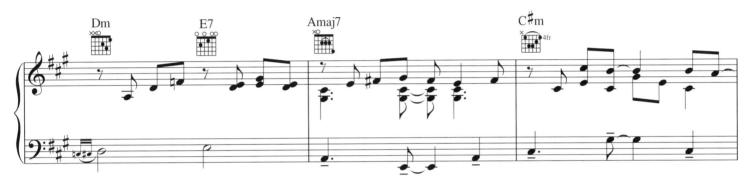

Well, I know it's kind of late. ____
know it's kind of strange ____
Instrumental solo

I hope I did - n't wake ____ you, but what I
but ev - 'ry time I'm near ____ you, I just

got to say can't wait. ___
run out of things to say. ___
I know you'd un - der - stand. _

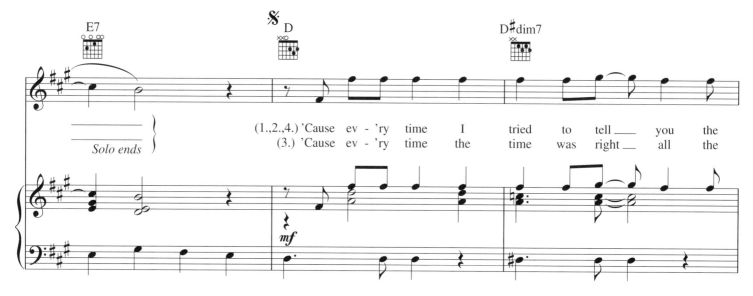

Solo ends

(1.,2.,4.) 'Cause ev - 'ry time I tried to tell ___ you the
(3.) 'Cause ev - 'ry time the time was right ___ all the

words just came out wrong. ___
words just came out wrong. ___
So I'll have to say ____ I love _
So I'll have to say ____ I love _

___ you in a song. _____
___ you in a song. ___

Yeah, I
Instrumental solo

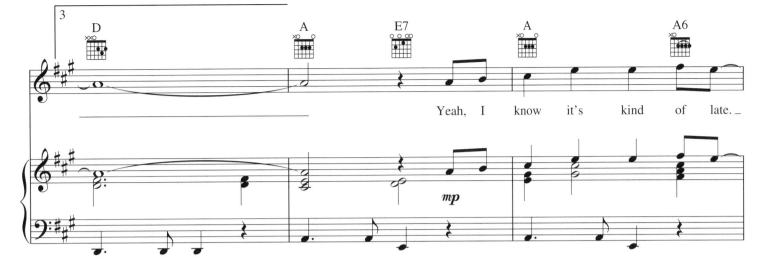

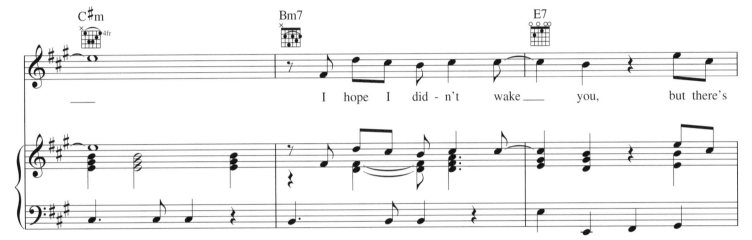

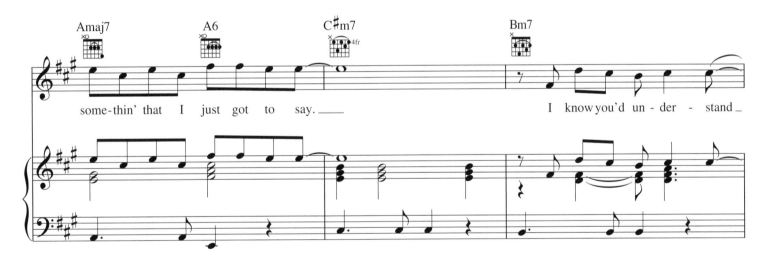

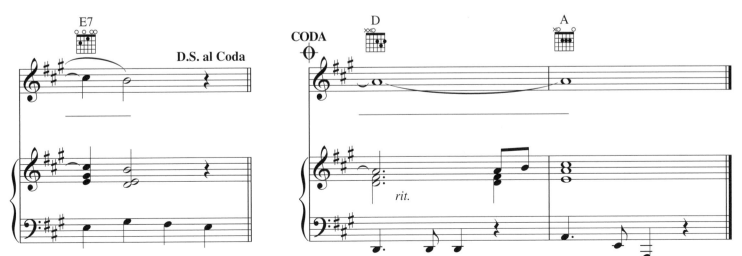

A GROOVY KIND OF LOVE

Words and Music by TONI WINE
and CAROLE BAYER SAGER

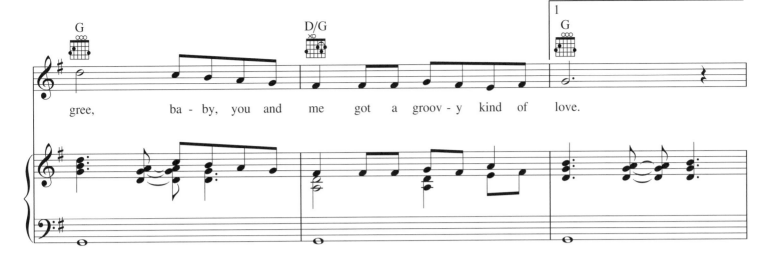

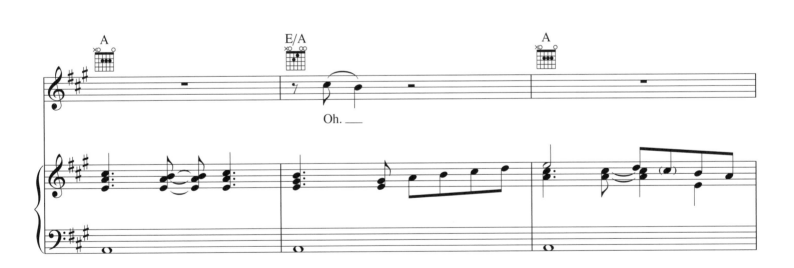

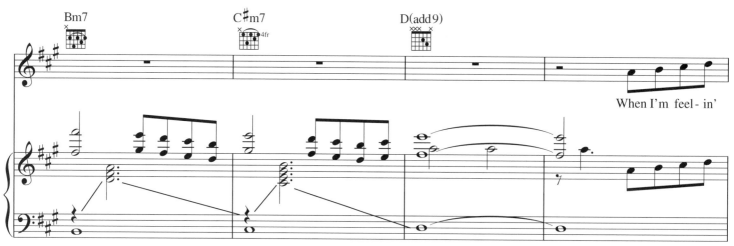

When I'm feel-in'

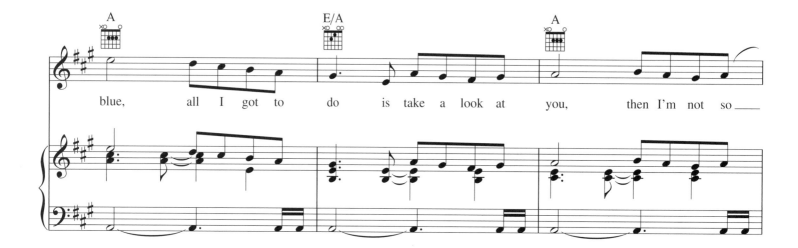

blue, all I got to do is take a look at you, then I'm not so

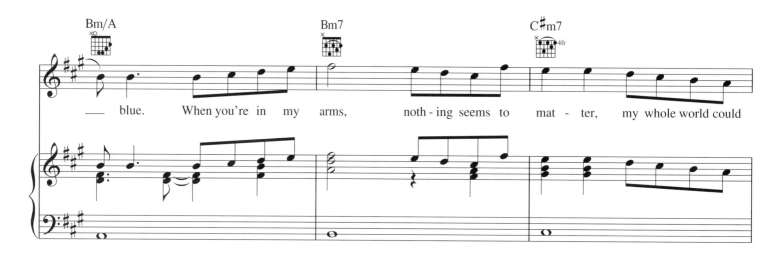

blue. When you're in my arms, noth-ing seems to mat-ter, my whole world could

shat-ter, I don't care. Would-n't you a-gree, baby, you and

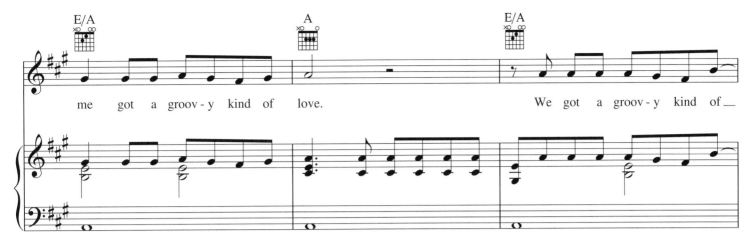

me got a groov-y kind of love.　　　We got a groov-y kind of

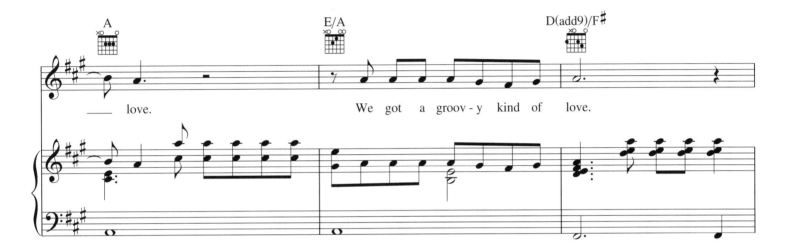

＿ love.　　We got a groov-y kind of love.

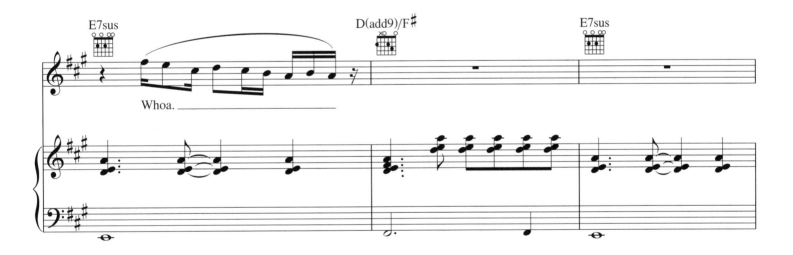

Whoa. ＿＿＿＿＿＿＿＿＿＿

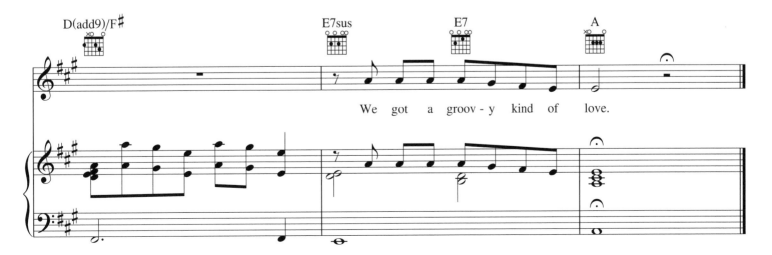

We got a groov-y kind of love.

HAPPY TOGETHER

Words and Music by GARRY BONNER
and ALAN GORDON

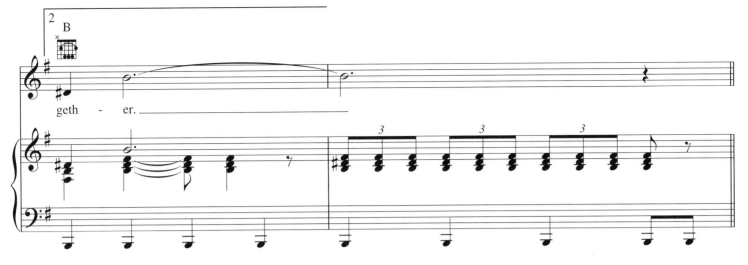

geth - er.

I can see me lov - in' no - bod - y but you for all my life.

When you're with me, ba - by, the skies -- 'll be

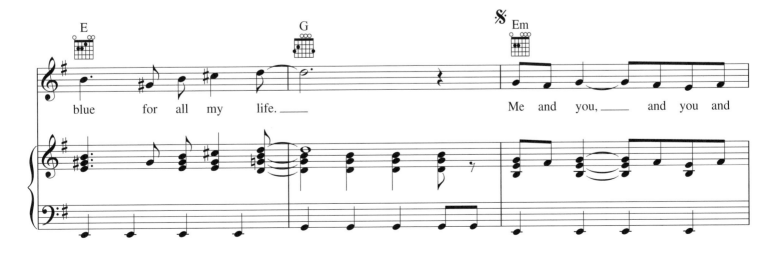

blue for all my life. Me and you, and you and

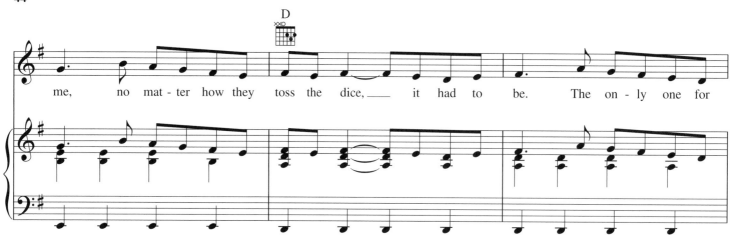

me, no mat-ter how they toss the dice,___ it had to be. The on-ly one for

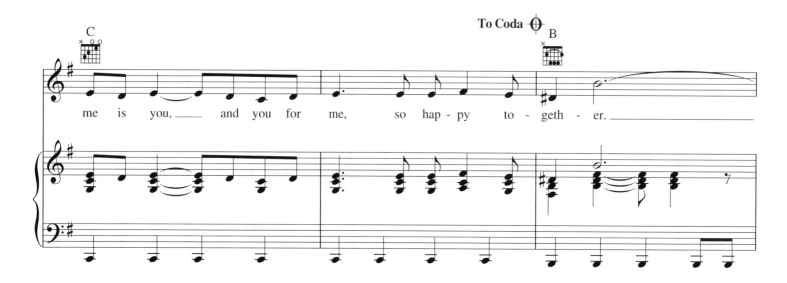

me is you,___ and you for me, so hap-py to-geth-er.___

Ba ba ba ba ba ba

ba ba ba ba ba.___ Ba ba ba ba

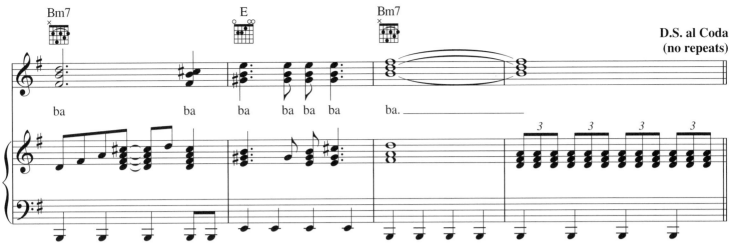

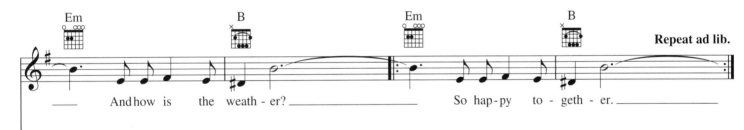

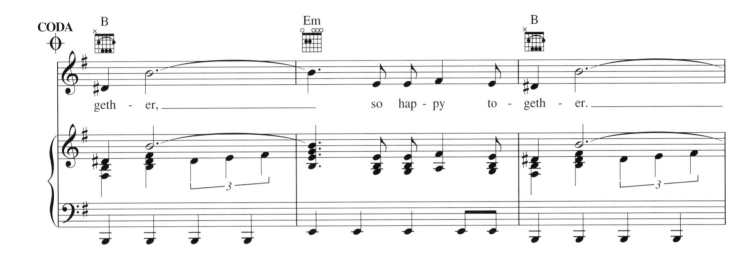

JUST THE WAY YOU ARE

Words and Music by
BILLY JOEL

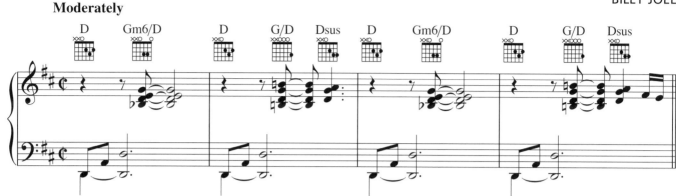

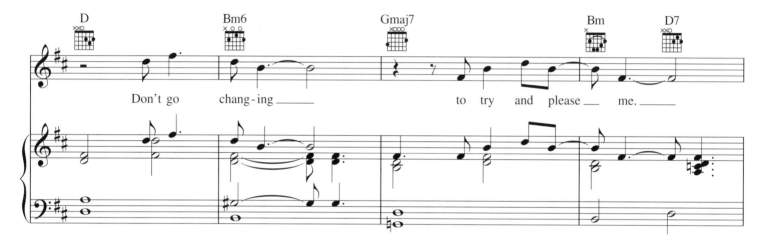

Don't go chang-ing _____ to try and please __ me. _____

You nev-er let me down __ be-fore. __ Mm, _____ mm. _____

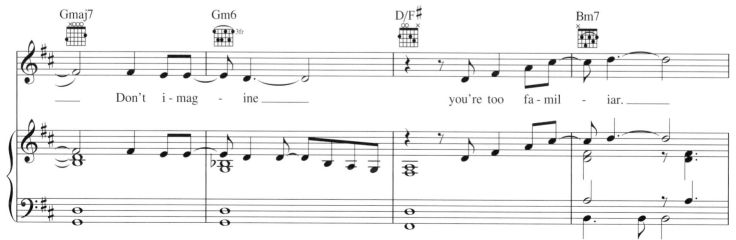

_____ Don't i-mag - ine _____ you're too fa-mil - iar. _____

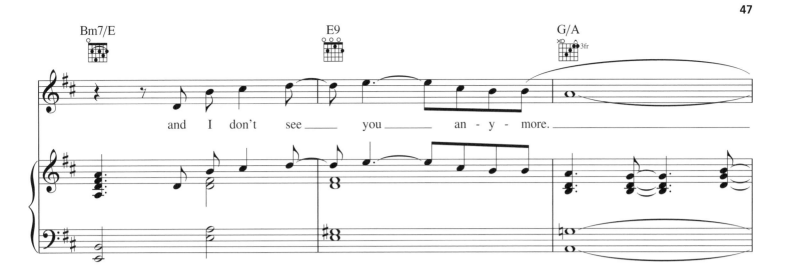

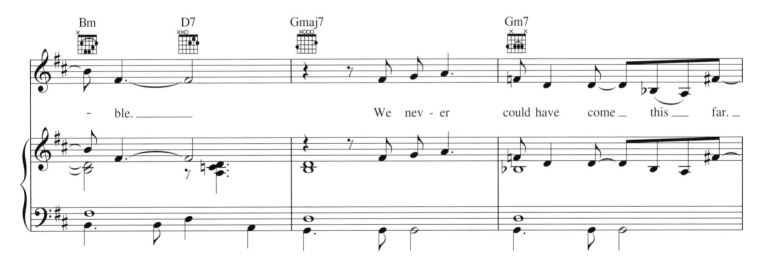

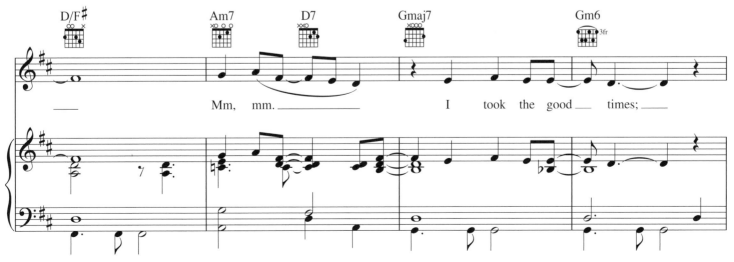

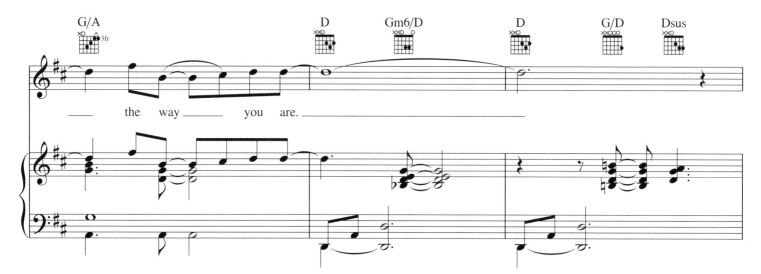

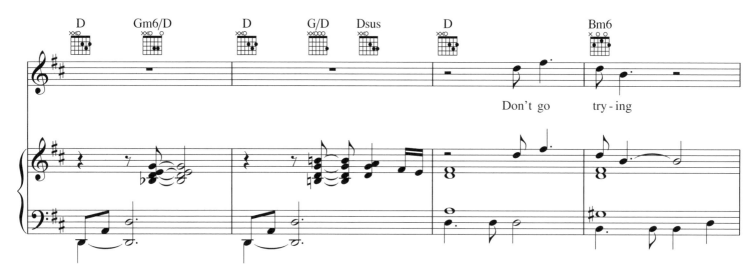

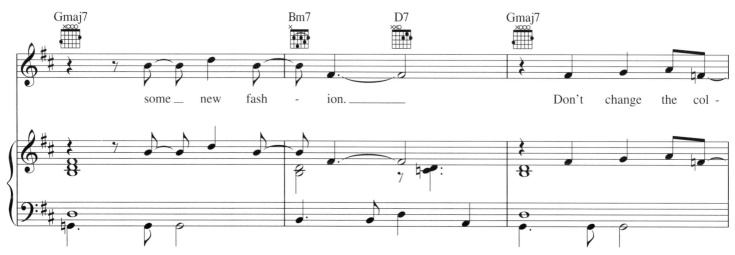

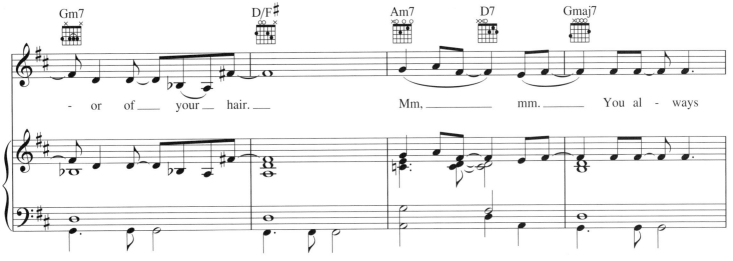

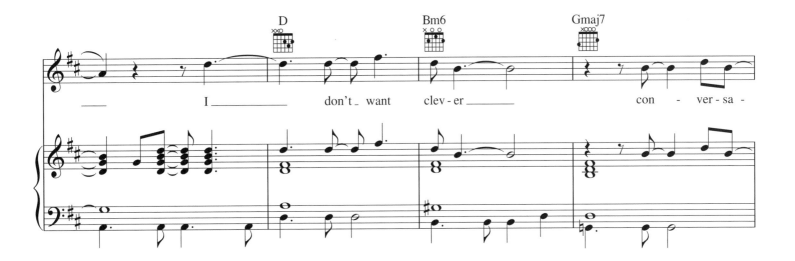

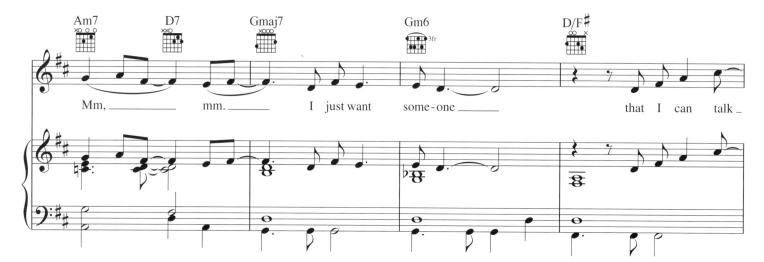

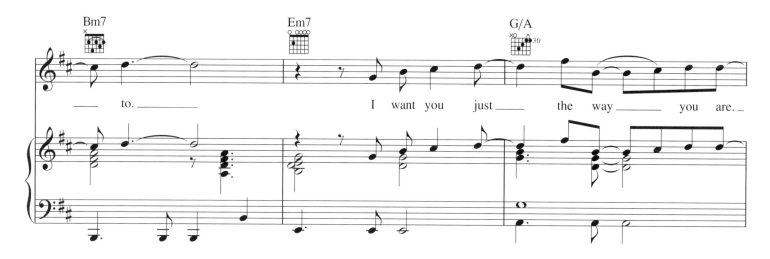

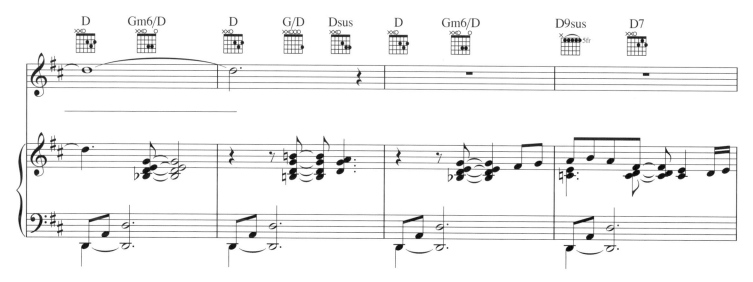

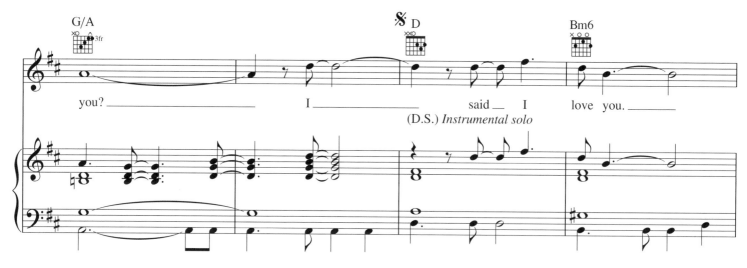

you?_____ I_____ said _ I love you._____

(D.S.) *Instrumental solo*

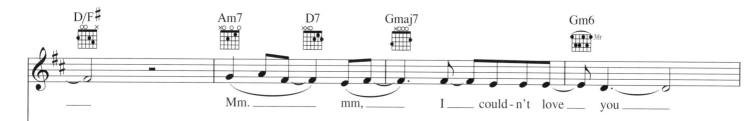

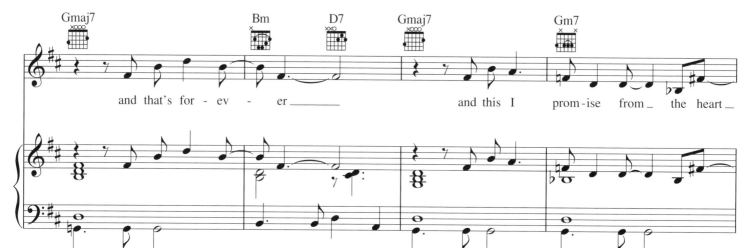

and that's for - ev - er _____ and this I prom-ise from _ the heart _____

Mm. _____ mm, _____ I __ could-n't love __ you _____

R.H.

To Coda ⊕

an - y bet - ter. _____ I love _ you just _

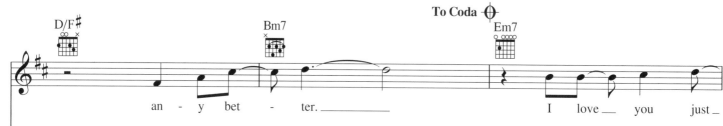

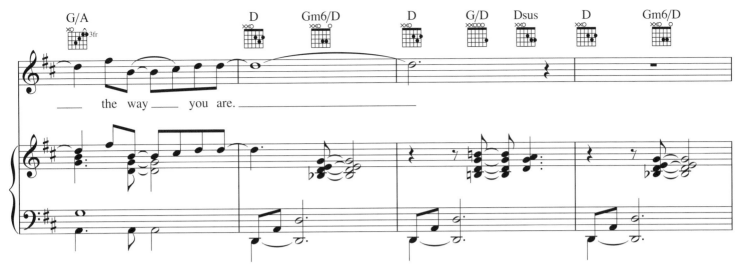

the way you are.

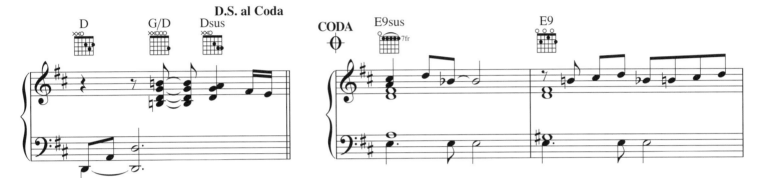

D.S. al Coda

CODA

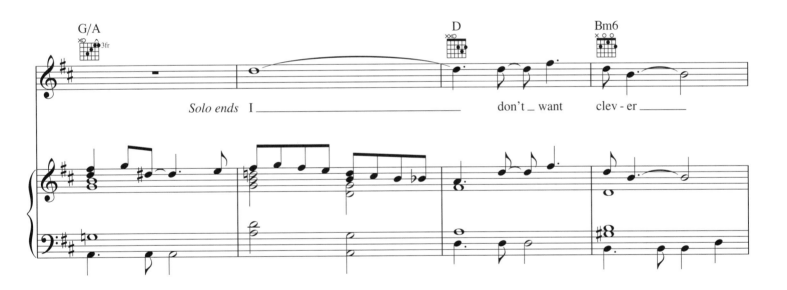

Solo ends I don't want clev-er

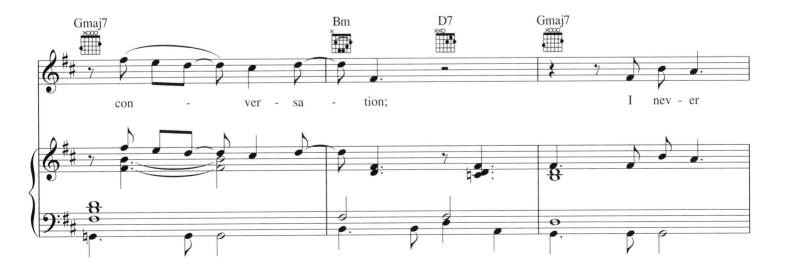

con - ver - sa - tion; I nev-er

MINUTE BY MINUTE

Words and Music by MICHAEL McDONALD
and LESTER ABRAMS

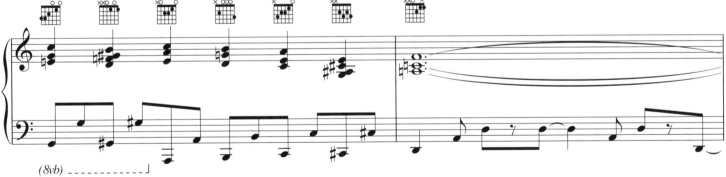

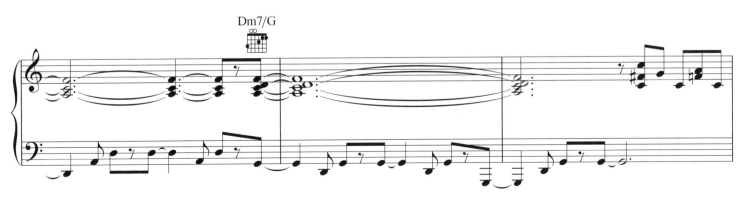

Hey, __ don't __ wor - ry; I've been lied _____ to.
You __ would __ stay just to watch me, dar - ling,

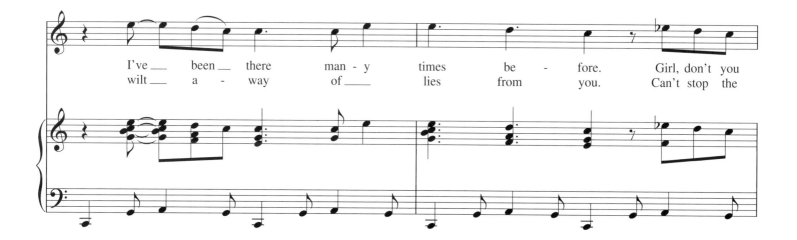

I've __ been __ there man - y times be - fore. Girl, don't you
wilt __ a - way of ____ lies from you. Can't stop the

wor - ry; I know where I stand. _____ I don't need __ this
hab - it of liv - ing on the run. _____ Take it all __ for

love; I don't need your hand. I know I _____ could
grant - ed, like you're the on - ly one. Liv - ing on _____ my

turn, think - ing you'd be gone, that I must be _____ pre -
own, some - how that sounds nice. You think I'm _____ your

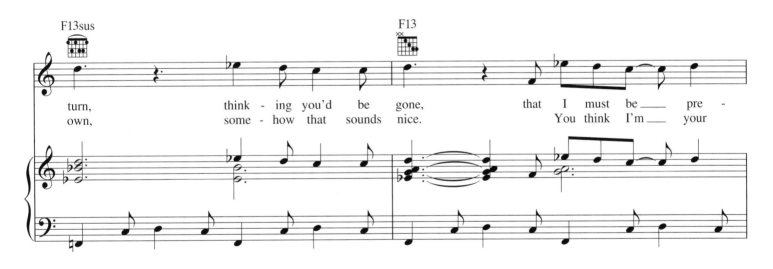

pared an - y - time to car - ry on, but
fool; well, __ you may just be right, 'cause

(min-ute   by   min-ute   by   min-ute   by   min-ute) I keep hold-ing   on. __

__ (I'll   be   hold-ing   on,   I'll   be   hold-ing

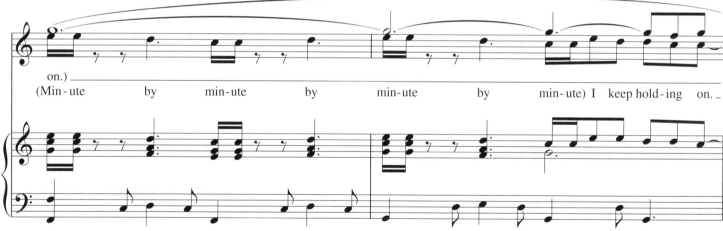

on.) ____
(Min-ute   by   min-ute   by   min-ute   by   min-ute) I keep hold-ing   on. __

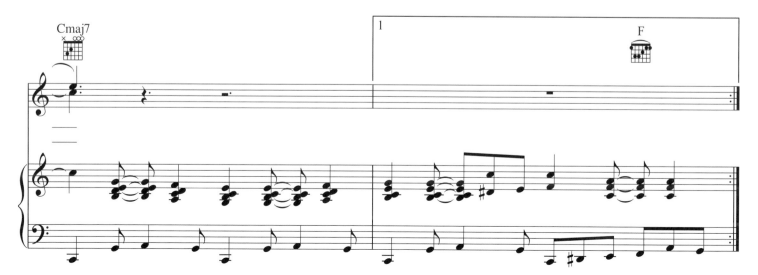

I keep hold- ing on.

Call my name _ and

I'll be gone. You reach out and I won't be _____ there.

Optional Ending

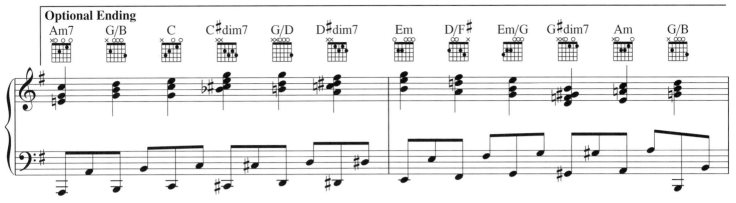

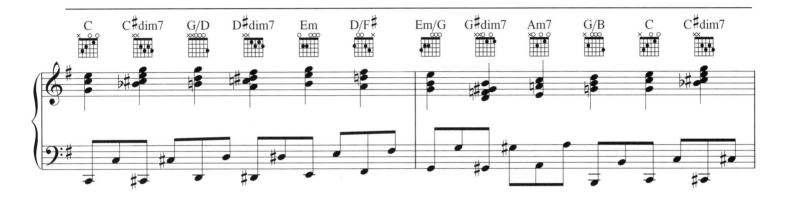

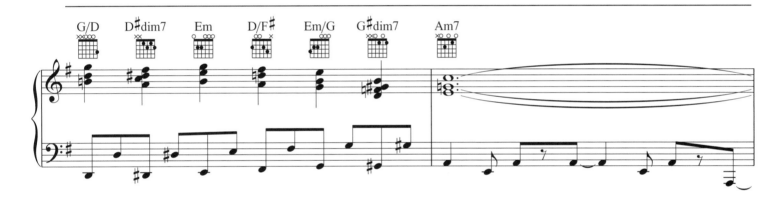

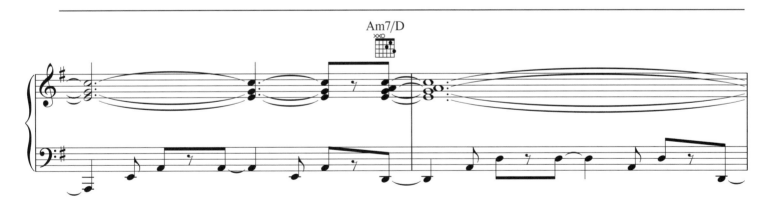

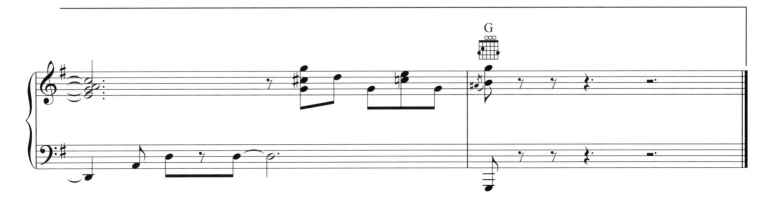

ON AND ON

Words and Music by
STEPHEN BISHOP

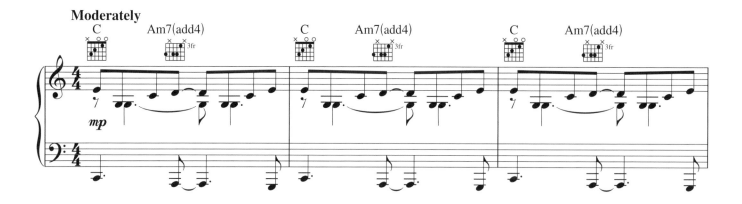

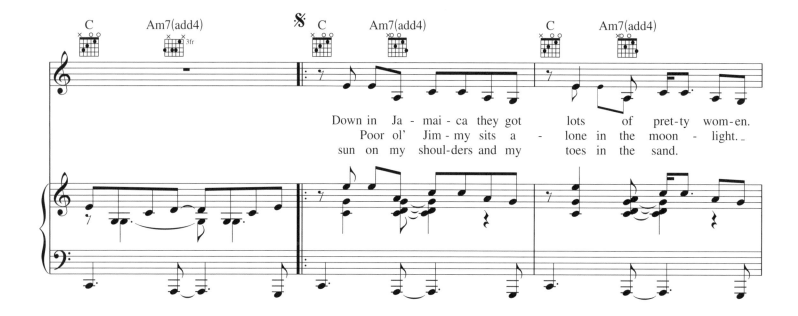

Down in Ja - mai - ca they got lots of pret-ty wom-en.
Poor ol' Jim - my sits a - lone in the moon - light.
sun on my shoul-ders and my toes in the sand.

Steal your mon - ey, then they break your heart. Lone - some Sue, she's in
Saw his wom - an kiss an - oth - er man. So he takes a lad - der; steals the
Wom - an's left me for some oth - er man. Ah, but I don't care. I'll just

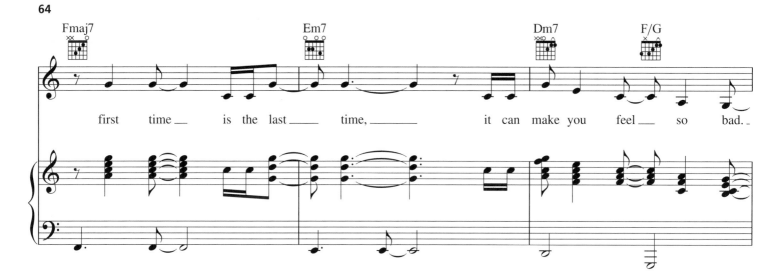

first time ___ is the last ___ time, ___ it can make you feel ___ so bad. ___

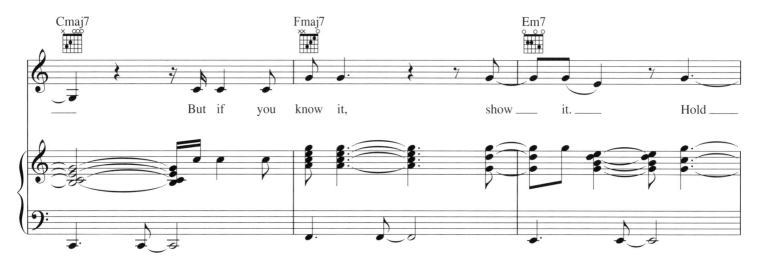

But if you know it, ___ show ___ it. ___ Hold ___

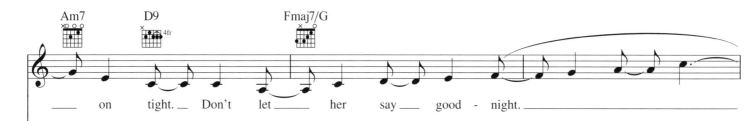

___ on tight. ___ Don't let ___ her say ___ good - night. ___

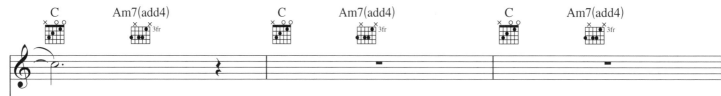

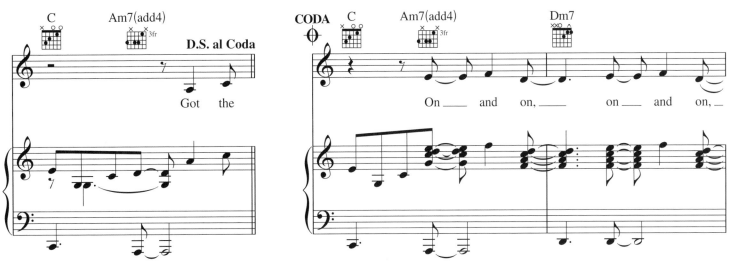

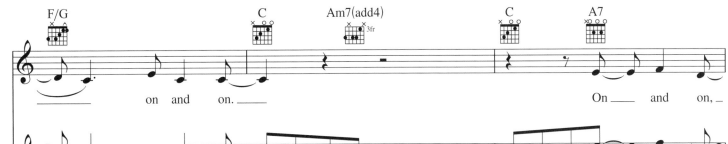

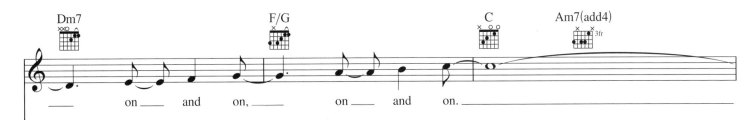

WE'VE GOT TONIGHT

Words and Music by
BOB SEGER

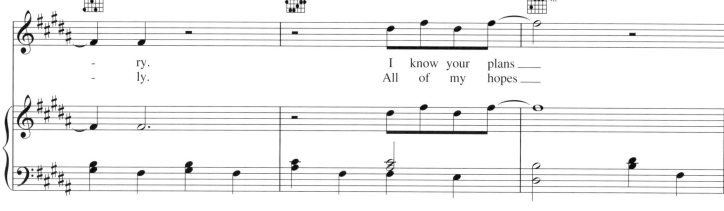

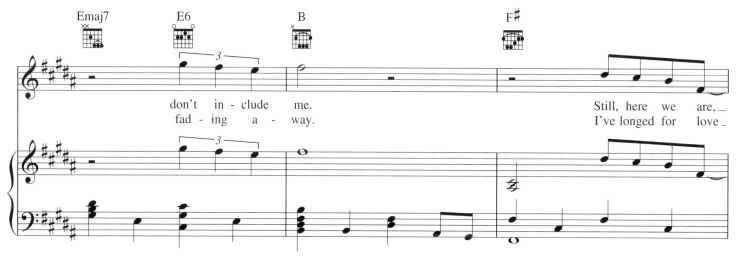

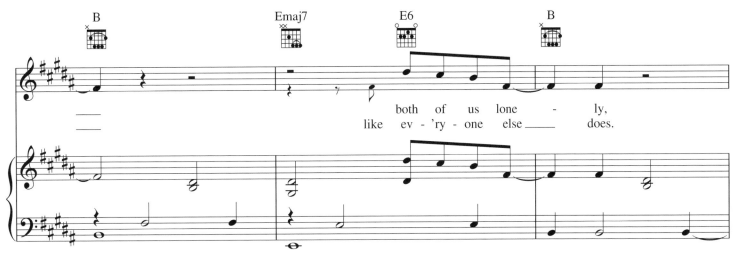

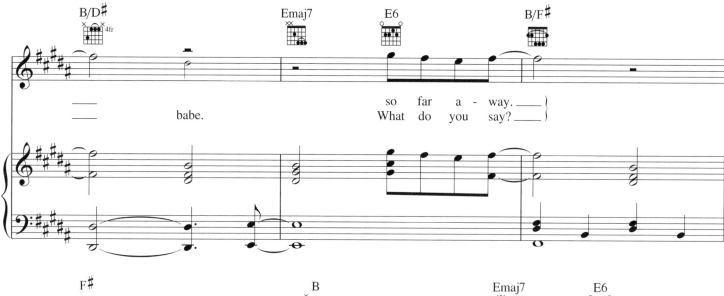

so far a-way.____
babe. What do you say?____

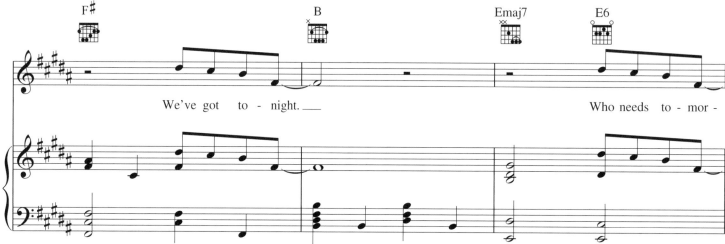

We've got to-night.____ Who needs to-mor-

- row? We've got to-night,____ babe.____

Why don't you stay.

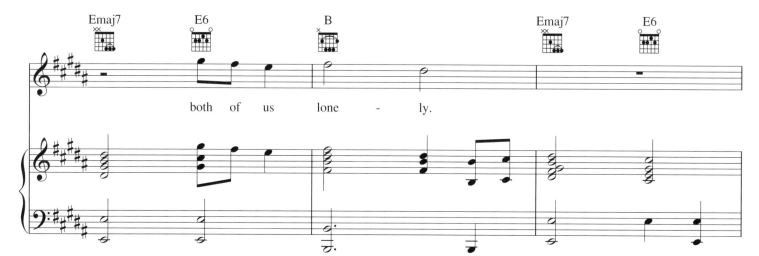

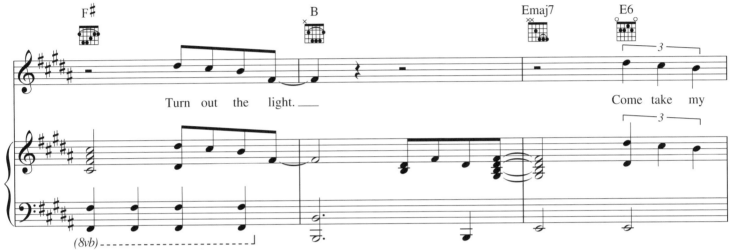

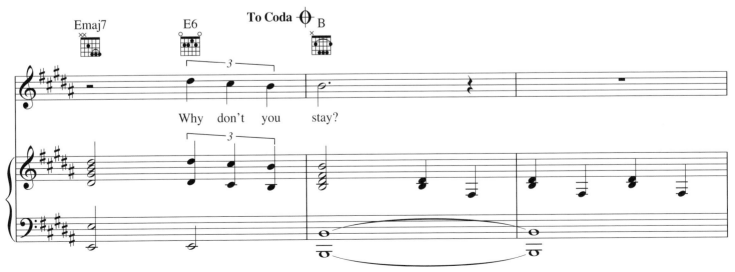

We've got to - night. ___

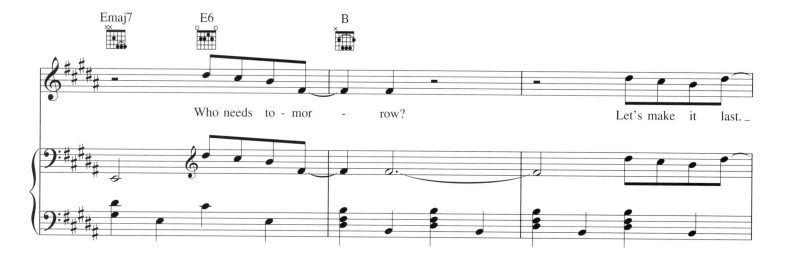

Who needs to - mor - row? Let's make it last. __

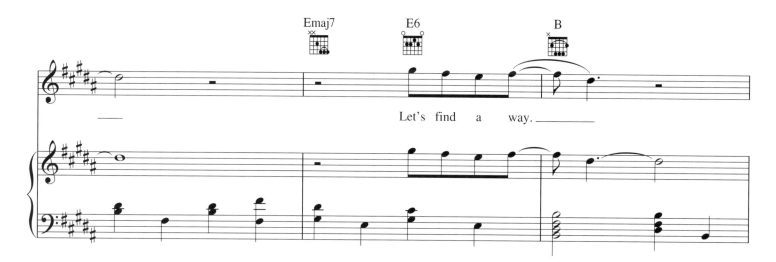

___ Let's find a way. _____

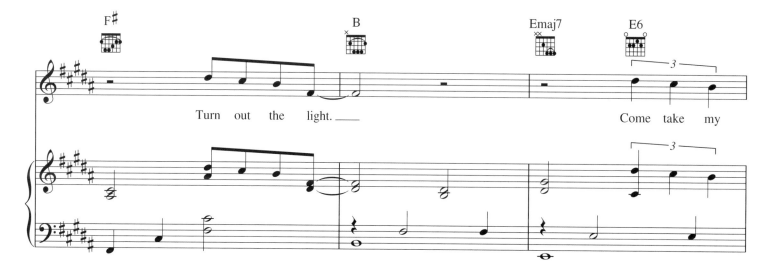

Turn out the light. ___ Come take my

hand now. We've got to-night,____ babe.

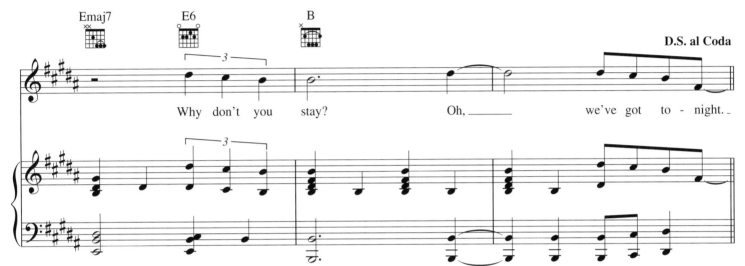

D.S. al Coda

Why don't you stay? Oh,_____ we've got to-night.__

CODA

stay?_____ Oh._____

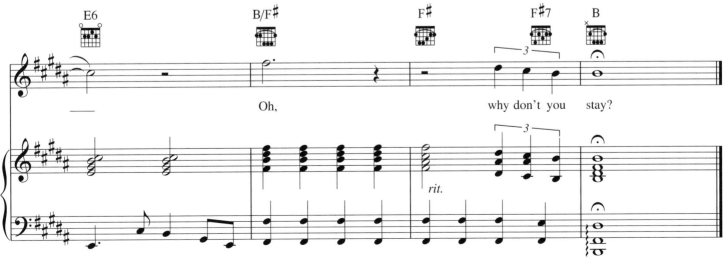

____ Oh, why don't you stay?

rit.

YOUR SONG

Words and Music by ELTON JOHN
and BERNIE TAUPIN

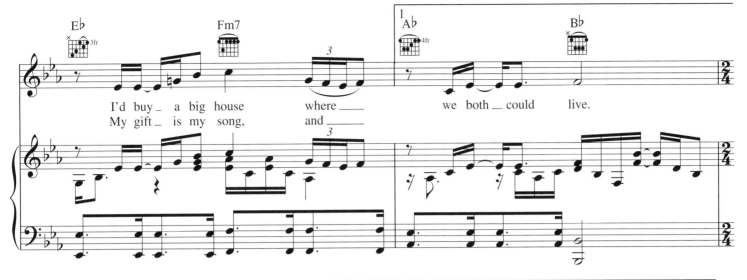

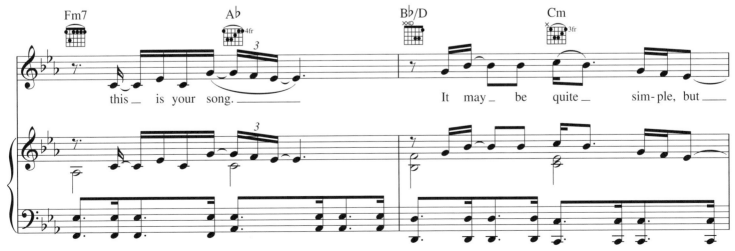

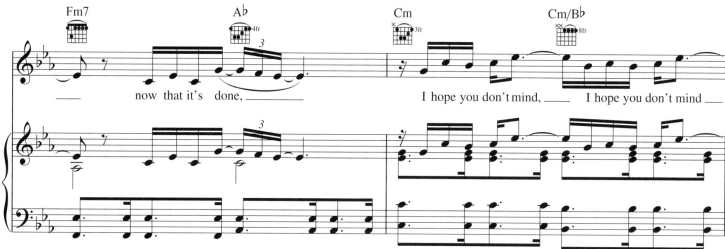

now that it's done, _____ I hope you don't mind, _____ I hope you don't mind _____

_____ that I put _____ down in _____ words how won-der-ful life is _____ while

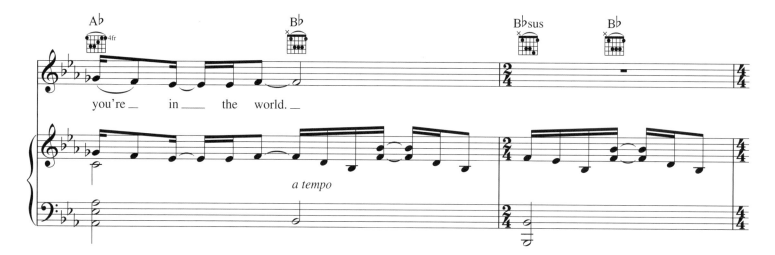

you're _____ in _____ the world. _____

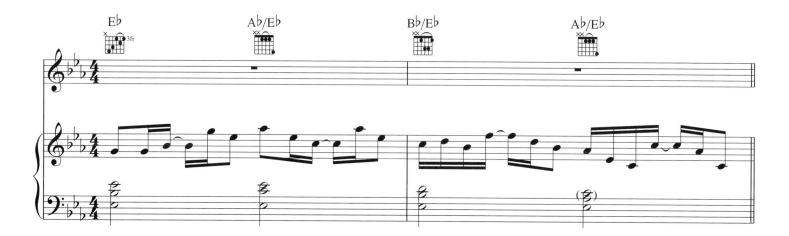

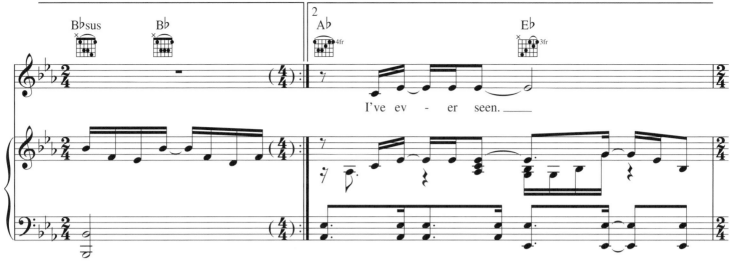

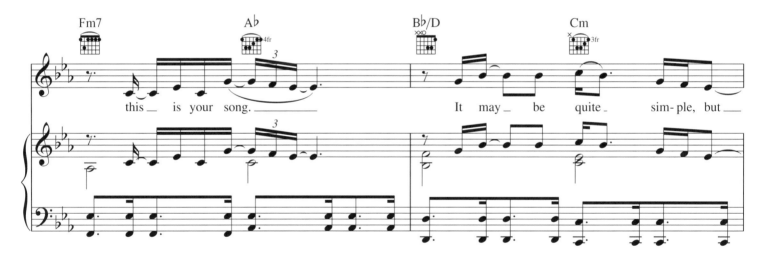

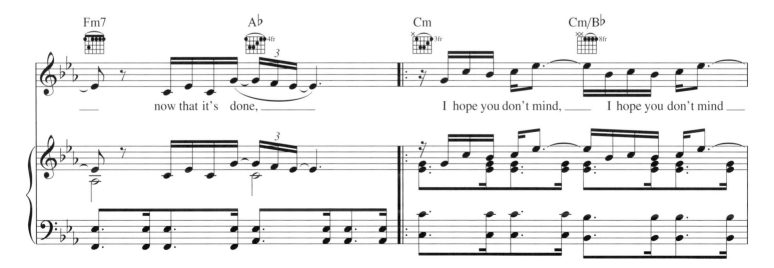

that I put down in words how won-der-ful life is while

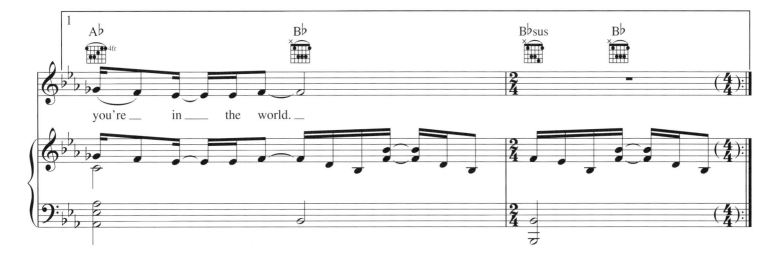

you're in the world.

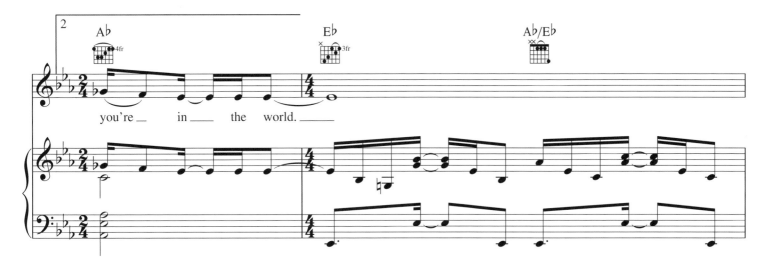

you're in the world.

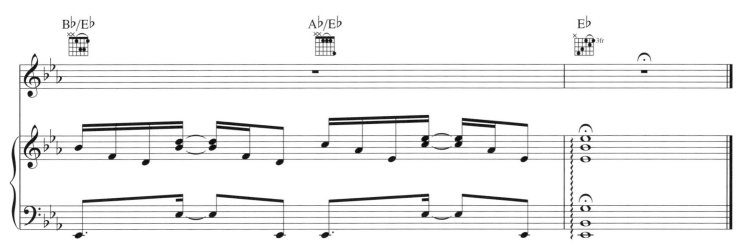

TOP OF THE WORLD

Words and Music by JOHN BETTIS
and RICHARD CARPENTER

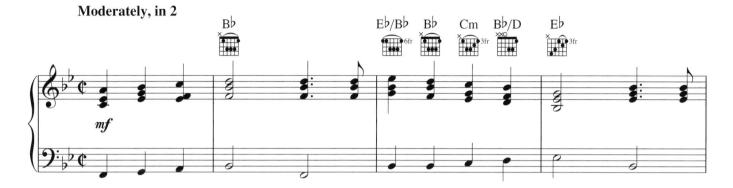

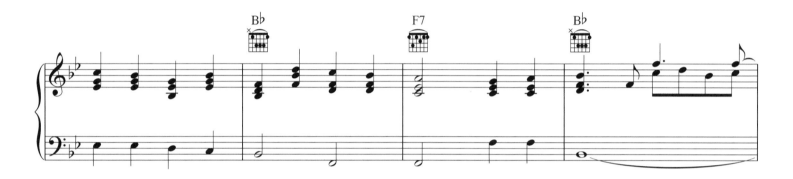

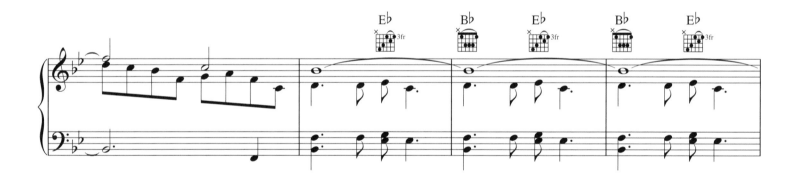

Such a feel - in's com - in' o - ver me. ___
Some - thing in ___ the wind has learned ___ my name. ___

There is won - der in ____ most
And it's tell - in' me ____ that

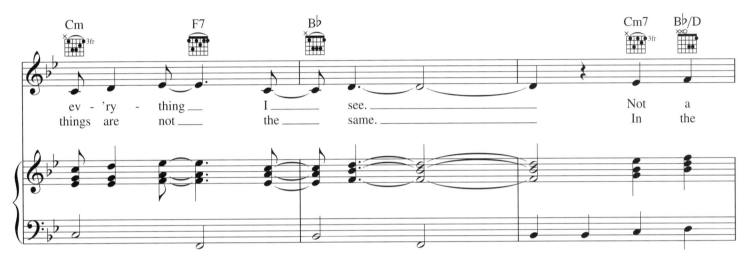

ev - 'ry - thing ____ I ____ see. ____ Not a
things are not ____ the ____ same. ____ In the

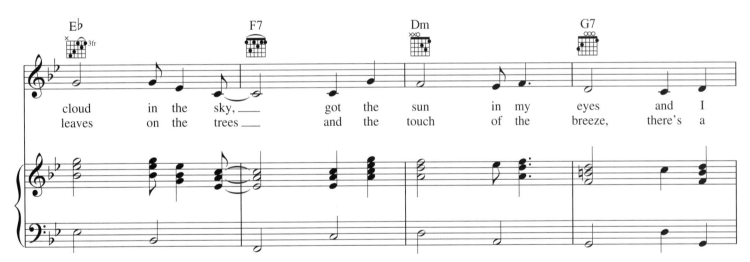

cloud in the sky, ____ got the sun in my eyes and I
leaves on the trees ____ and the sun touch of the eyes breeze, there's a

won't be sur - prised ____ if it's a dream. ____
pleas - in' sense of hap - pi - ness for me. ____

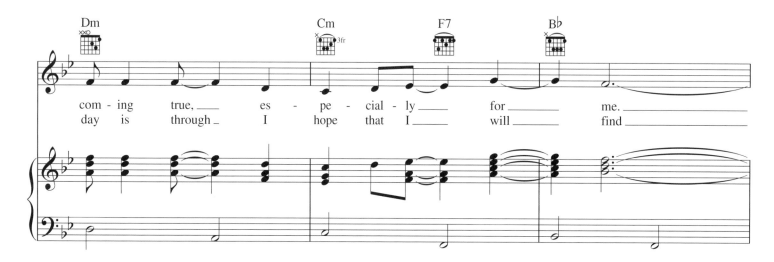

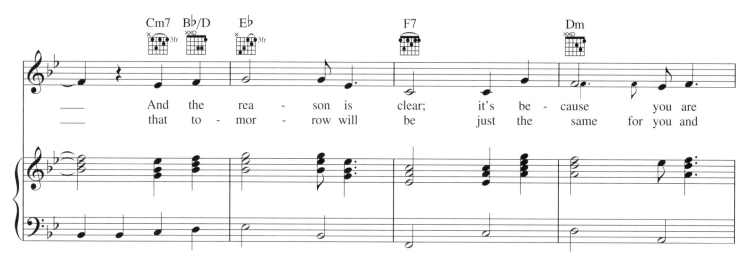

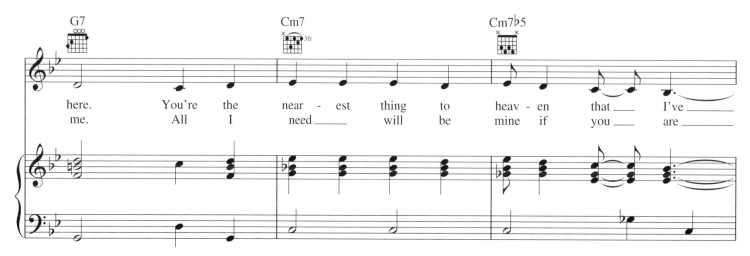

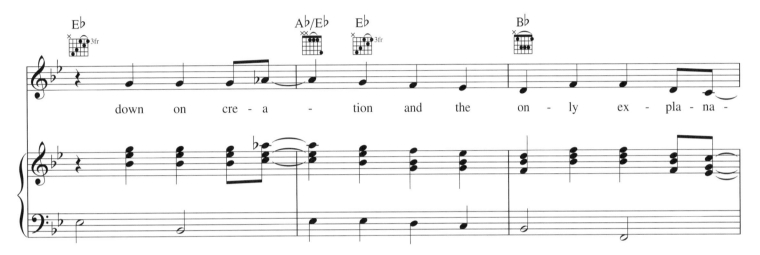

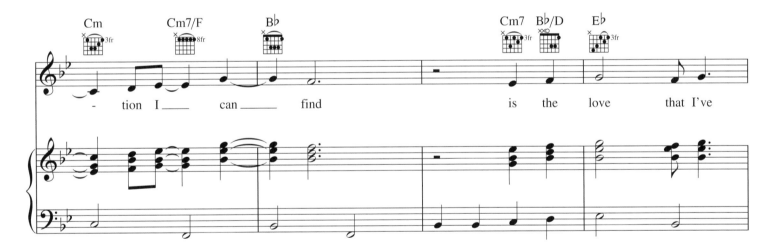

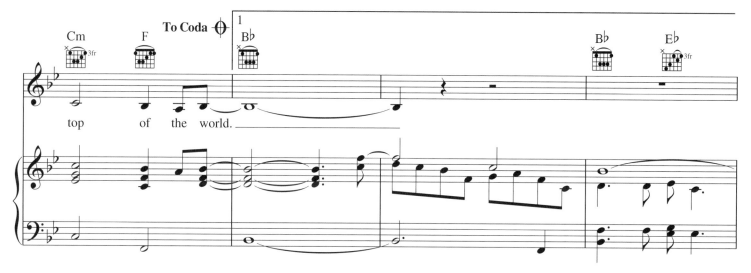

top of the world.

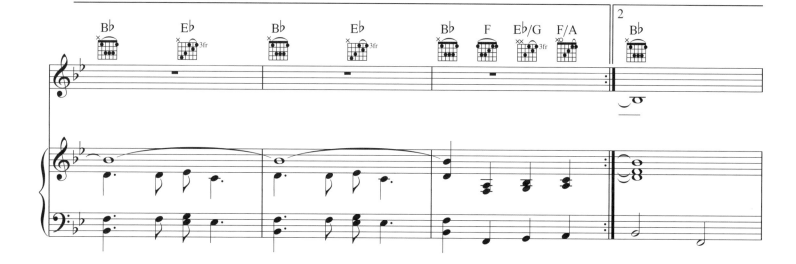

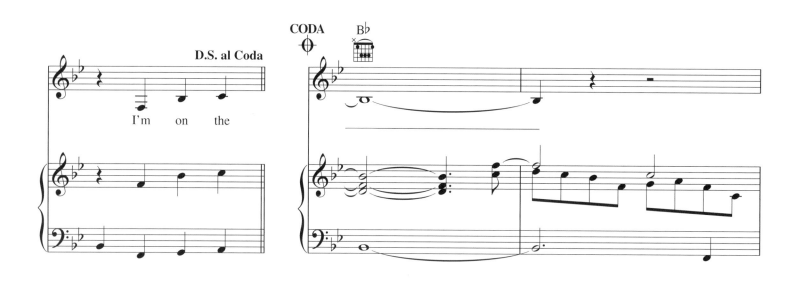

D.S. al Coda

I'm on the

CODA

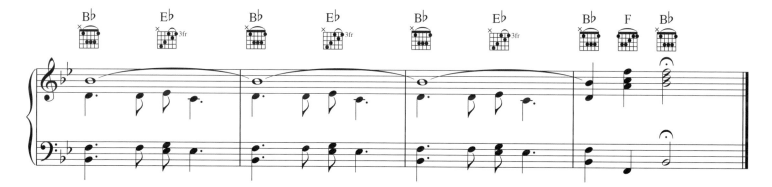

Community and the Global Family

The songs in the following section all take a broader view, addressing such themes

as community, family, and global love. From the harmonious world

envisioned in John Lennon's "Imagine" to the delightful one observed in

Louis Armstrong's "What a Wonderful World," these are the

songs that continue to inspire in turbulent times.

All You Need Is Love (page 90)

The Beatles' "All You Need Is Love" was first heard, fittingly, during the Summer of Love, on June 25, 1967. The British Broadcasting Corporation commissioned the song for *Our World* — a live international television program, the first of its type. On that historic broadcast, The Beatles played the song along with some of their good friends, including members of the Rolling Stones, Eric Clapton, and others. At the turbulent time of its release, "All You Need Is Love" was intended to contain a simple message of hope for all people. And now, more than four decades later, it retains its universal message about the primacy of love.

While "All You Need Is Love" is fairly straightforward, the song has got some sneaky changes in meter. For instance, beginning in bar 5 the song alternates between 3/4 and 4/4 time signatures over the course of several measures. So be sure to count the beats of these bars carefully; if necessary use a metronome so that you'll avoid letting the pulse slip while changing time signatures. Another technical note: in bar 3, where you see the *trill* sign, (⁓) rapidly alternate between the primary note (A) and the note above (B), ending with the cue-sized notes. If you find this too difficult to articulate, just omit it and play only the quarter note A.

American Pie (page 98)

"American Pie," by the singer-songwriter Don McLean, was purportedly inspired by "The Day the Music Died" — February 3, 1959, when the rockers Buddy Holly, Ritchie Valens, and the Big Bopper were tragically killed in a plane crash following a concert. Released in 1971, "American Pie" is also about a certain loss of innocence, both in music and in politics, during the '60s. But the song is quite playful, with colorful lyrics rife with musical references, like "sergeants played a marching tune" (The Beatles' "Sgt. Pepper's Lonely Hearts Club Band") and "eight miles high and falling fast" (The Byrds' "Eight Miles High"). Most important, "American Pie" has had lasting appeal as part of our musical cultural heritage.

Arranged here in the key of G major and with a dearth of accidentals, "American Pie" is fairly easy to play. While quite long, it's essentially comprised of a couple of repeating sections; in other words, there's not as much music to learn as it would appear. If you don't feel like playing the entire song, simply omit some of the repeats, as did radio deejays when the song first came out. If you choose to play the whole tune, though, you'll want to make sure to vary the dynamics throughout, to avoid monotony. Start off by playing the music up until the first repeat in a very laid-back and free manner. Then, when you get to the repeat, play in a more rhythmic, measured way. On each repetition, get a little faster and louder; then, after you work through the fourth ending, when you get to the music marked *Freely*, resume the feel you used to start the piece.

Come Together (page 95)

The Beatles' "Come Together" has a special distinction; it's a rock song that was originally written for a gubernatorial campaign; Timothy Leary's failed 1969 race in California against Ronald Reagan. The song, which ended up as the opening track on The Beatles album *Abbey Road* (1969), became one of the group's most popular tunes. With its swampy bass line and minimal chord work, "Come Together" is one of the most bluesy songs in this collection — and is quite satisfying to play on the piano.

Written in D minor, "Come Together" has a double-time feeling — twice as fast as written, with eighth notes sounding like quarter notes, 16ths like eighths, and so on. Cleverly, the left-hand piano part is a composite arrangement of some of the bass and guitar parts heard on the original recording. In bar 1 and appearing throughout much of the song is Paul McCartney's heavy bass line; make sure you've got that part down before you play the rest of the tune. In bar 9 and elsewhere is an essential rhythm-guitar move, a type of shuffle pattern originally played by boogie-woogie pianists and later made standard for guitar by players like Chuck Berry. Instead of a plain old A chord, the pattern moves between two-note A5 (A–E) and A6 (A–F#) chords. In a rock 'n' roll song, you can plug in this handy pattern wherever you see a major chord.

Fly Like an Eagle (page 108)

The American rocker Steve Miller first recorded "Fly Like an Eagle" in 1973. But his second version, released on the 1976 album of the same name, is better known. This soaring song, no pun intended, became one of Miller's signature numbers; he still plays it often in concert, giving his band a chance to stretch out on long improvisations. The song has also found its way into other contexts, including the 1996 movie *Space Jam* and, appropriately enough, commercials for the United States Postal Service, whose logo is an eagle.

"Fly Like an Eagle" is in the key of A minor. The original synthesizer intro (known as "Space Intro") is omitted in this arrangement. However, the first 4 bars of the bass clef contain the original guitar riff; be sure to play it with your right hand as indicated. In bar 5 and elsewhere, the X noteheads in the vocal line call for the words to be spoken, not sung. Being a jam-type song, "Fly like an Eagle" would give you an excellent chance to try your hand at improvisation. Here's a fun suggestion: Repeat the bass line in bars 5-8 while making up melodies based on the A natural minor scale (A–B–C–D–E–F–G) or the A Dorian mode (A–B–C–D–E–F#–G).

From a Distance (page 114)

In the mid-1980s a young singer-songwriter named Julie Gold was working in New York City as a secretary at HBO and writing songs in her spare time. She penned "From a Distance," about a loving and beneficent God, and in 1987 had the good fortune of having the song recorded by the singer-songwriter Nanci Griffith. A number of other renditions followed, the most famous of which the great vocalist Bette Middler released in 1990. "From a Distance" became an international hit, perhaps in part due to its coinciding with the first Persian Gulf War — a time when the song's hopeful message was particularly resonant, especially for soldiers and their families.

You'll want to play "From a Distance" (written in G major), at a pretty slow tempo and with great feeling. Pay careful attention to the rhythms throughout, particularly 32nd notes, two notes in the space of one 16th note. You might have noticed the (add2) chords throughout. These chords are simply major triads with an added second. So, G(add2), for example, is a G triad (G–B–D) with an A. That single note adds a poignant feel to the chord.

Imagine (page 124)

"Imagine" (1971) is a wonderful song that John Lennon wrote not long after The Beatles disbanded in 1970. The song dealt with all that Lennon was dreaming about at the time — one country, one world, one people. It ranks up there with any of the great songs that Lennon wrote with Paul McCartney for The Beatles. "Imagine" is also one of the most influential songs of all time. In fact, in a 2006 interview on National Public Radio, former United States President Jimmy Carter observed that in his extensive travels around the globe he'd heard the song at the same frequency as national anthems.

Shown here in the original key of C major, "Imagine" should be played slowly and with a lot of feeling. The first four bars contain the song's signature riff, the chord progression of which forms the bulk of the piece, so make sure you've got this part down before proceeding with the rest of the song. Note, too, that the right hand plays notes in the bass clef here. One element that gives "Imagine" an especially sweet sound is the use of the C major seventh (Cmaj7) chord — a C major triad (C–E–G) with an added seventh (B), a sound more commonly heard in jazz. Listen to the difference in mood created when you add just that one note to the C chord.

Somewhere Out There (page 119)

"Somewhere Out There" is a song about familial love, in particular, that between two siblings. The tune was first heard in the 1986 animated film *An American Tail*, an immigration story set in late 1800s Russia and New York. It was sung by the characters Fievel and Tillie, brother and sister mice, who, facing impending separation, expressed hopes of being reunited. "Somewhere Out There" also appeared in the movie's closing credits, as a duet by Linda Ronstadt and James Ingram. It was this version that became a huge international hit and remains wildly popular.

Play "Somewhere Out There," arranged in C major, at a moderate tempo and with considerable expressiveness. At the beginning of the song, you'll note the indication "*With pedal.*" This calls for you to use the sustain pedal (on the far right) with your right foot. As you've probably noticed, this pedal allows for all of the notes on the piano to sustain after the keys have been played. In playing this song, don't keep the pedal depressed throughout, for that will cause the music to sound like a great mess. Rather, experiment with changing the pedal as the chords change, so that only the desired music rings together.

We Are Family (page 128)

Formed in the early 1970s, Sister Sledge was a disco group of singing siblings — Kim, Debbie, Joni, and Kathy Sledge. The group's most well known song is "We Are Family" (1979), a celebration of the ties that bind a family together. Now one of the most popular dance numbers of all time, "We Are Family" has been heard in some pretty important contexts, such as the 1979 theme song for the Pittsburgh Pirates and at the 2004 National Democratic Convention. And for the last thirty years it has been played at countless weddings, reunions, and other family functions.

Play "We Are Family," presented here in the key of B♭ major, at an upbeat dance tempo, striving for a funky feel. As you play through the song you might wonder what makes it sound so soulful. There are a couple of reasons for this: First, the melody makes use of a *blue note* — the flatted seventh, in this case, the note A♭. This simple adjustment makes things nice and funky — try singing the melody with an A natural instead to hear the difference. Blue notes are also found in the song's chords. A B♭7 chord is a B♭ triad (B♭–D–F) with a flatted seventh (A♭); an A♭7 chord is an A♭ triad (A♭–C–E♭) with a flatted seventh (G♭). Again, if you omit the blue notes from these chords, everything will sound a bit "vanilla."

We Are the World (page 136)

"We Are the World" was released in 1985 as a benefit single for victims of famine in Africa. The artists Michael Jackson and Lionel Richie wrote the song, and they sang it along with a super-group (called USA for Africa) of their fellow luminaries, including Paul Simon, Bruce Springsteen, and Stevie Wonder, among many others. The song quickly became the top-selling single in recorded history, and as of 2009 had raised more than sixty-three million dollars in humanitarian aid. Twenty-five years after the original release a remake (organized by Richie and Quincy Jones) was recorded to benefit the victims of the January 12, 2010 earthquake in Haiti. "We Are the World" remains extremely popular, its compassionate message still resonating throughout the world.

"We Are the World" starts off in the rich key of E major. The left hand, filled with whole and half notes, is easy to play. The right hand, though, is filled with 16th-note syncopations, so you might want to learn that part separately, remembering to subdivide throughout. A couple other things to be aware of: In the treble clef of bar 1, the squiggly line with the arrow calls for you to quickly roll the chord from the lowest note to the highest. Feel free to add this rolled treatment to other chords in the piece. Also, heads up on the key change, up a half step, to F major, on the last page. This move adds a dramatic feel to the piece.

What a Wonderful World (page 142)

As an improviser, the great jazz trumpeter Louis Armstrong was at his most vital in the 1920s. But he's best known for his 1968 recording of the song "What a Wonderful World." During the racially and politically tumultuous times of the late 1960s, the song struck an optimistic note, encouraging people to find the beauty and harmony in their everyday surroundings. Now a popular standard, "What a Wonderful World" has been covered by a stylistically diverse array of singers — everyone from blues musician B.B. King to punk rocker Joey Ramone.

"What a Wonderful World" is written here in the key of F major. You'll want to play the song, with its gently rolling eighth-note triplets (three per beat) in the left hand, at a very moderate tempo. The song has got a bunch of accidentals, so be sure to scan ahead for them as you play. In bars 9 and 10 are a couple of symbols that might be unfamiliar: a *crescendo* (<) sign in bar 9 and a *decrescendo* (>) in bar 10. As indicated, get louder through bar 9, and quieter in bar 10. Feel free to add some similar dynamics throughout the rest of the piece. One more thing — as for the indication *Rubato* at the end of the penultimate system, play very freely, speeding up or slowing down according to your own discretion.

What the World Needs Now Is Love (page 146)

The composer Burt Bacharach and lyricist Hal David are one of America's greatest songwriting teams. In the 1960s, they wrote a great number of tunes together in New York City's famous Brill Building. David, who lived on Long Island at the time, got the lyric ideas for "What the World Needs Now Is Love" when he was driving into the city for work, and as he usually did, Bacharach set the lyrics to a gorgeous melody and sophisticated chord progression. Most often, Bacharach and David would have the phenomenal singer Dionne Warwick record their songs. However, she happened to pass on this one, and instead it became a hit in 1965 for Jackie DeShannon. Forty-five years later the optimistic song still strikes a chord with listeners throughout the world.

Arranged here in the key of E minor (ending in G major), "What the World Needs Now Is Love" is a jazz waltz, so play it at a danceable tempo, counting "one, two, three; one, two, three, etc." throughout and emphasizing the first beat of each bar. At the same time, be sure to swing the eighth notes. A nice touch is the use of jazzy harmony; minor seventh and other fancy chords throughout. A minor seventh (m7) chord is simply a minor triad with the addition of a flatted seventh. So, a Bm7 chord is spelled: B–D–F#–A; an Em7: E–G–B–D. To best hear the flavor imparted by these chords, try playing the music with just triads, Bm (B–D–F#) and Em (E–G–B), and then listen to the difference the minor seventh makes.

Wouldn't It Be Nice (page 149)

The Beach Boys' 1966 *Pet Sounds* is one of the most influential pop albums ever made. On that record, The Beach Boys really pushed the envelope in terms of orchestration and arrangement, with richly layered vocal harmonies and all kinds of exotic instruments. Of course, a large part of the reason why *Pet Sounds* is so remarkable is that it has great songs, one of the most popular of which is "Wouldn't It Be Nice." This lovely tune still sounds fresh more than forty years after it was recorded.

"Wouldn't It Be Nice" is arranged here in the key of C major. A single-note bass part in the left hand and a melody with straightforward block chords in the right hand makes this tune easy to play. But it may be a little tricky to achieve the right rhythmic feel. If you play the music exactly as written, it could sound just a little stiff. In order to sound relaxed and swinging like this song calls for, it'd be a good idea to listen closely to the original version, and try playing along with it. For in music, you see, there are often things that defy notation.

ALL YOU NEED IS LOVE

Words and Music by JOHN LENNON
and PAUL McCARTNEY

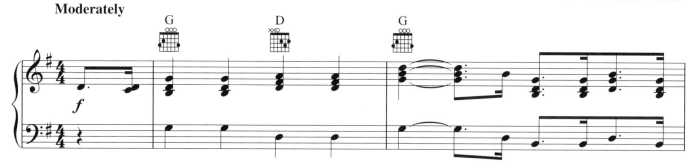

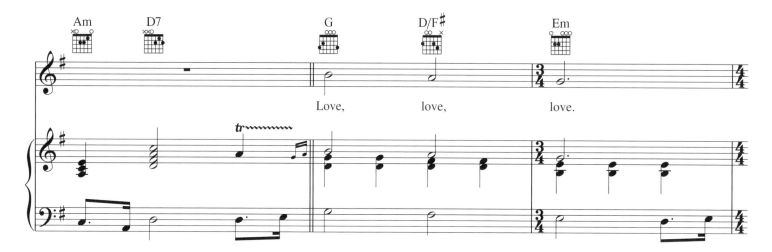

Love,   love,   love.

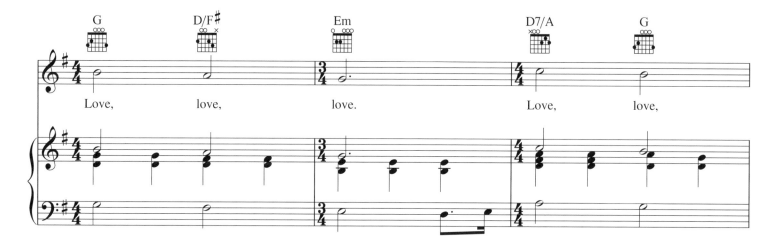

Love,   love,   love.   Love,   love,

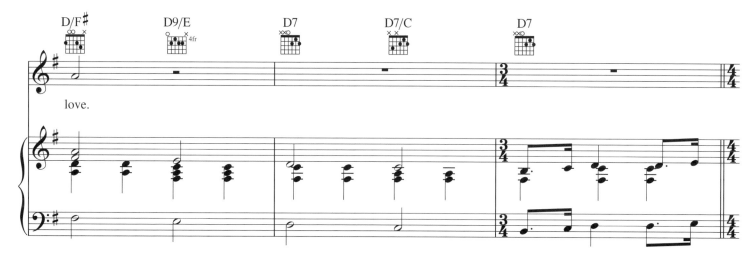

love.

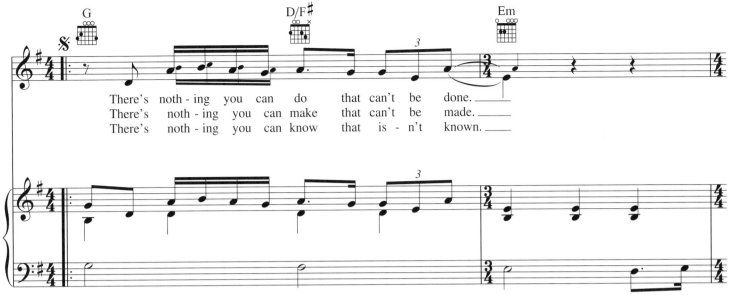

There's noth-ing you can do that can't be done. ____
There's noth-ing you can make that can't be made. ____
There's noth-ing you can know that is-n't known. ____

Noth-ing you can sing that can't be sung. ____
No one you can save that can't be saved. ____
Noth-ing you can see that is-n't shown. ____

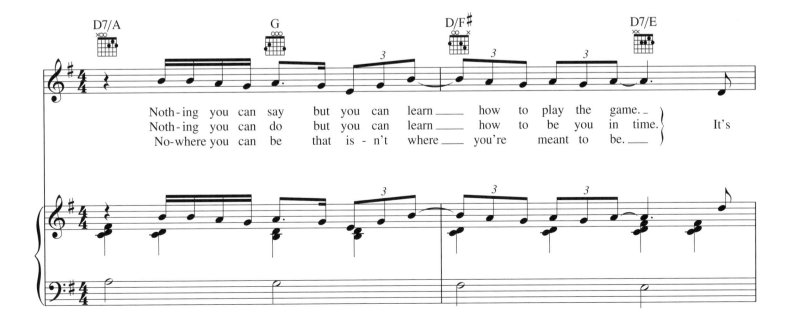

Noth-ing you can say but you can learn ____ how to play the game. ____
Noth-ing you can do but you can learn ____ how to be you in time. } It's
No-where you can be that is-n't where ____ you're meant to be. ____

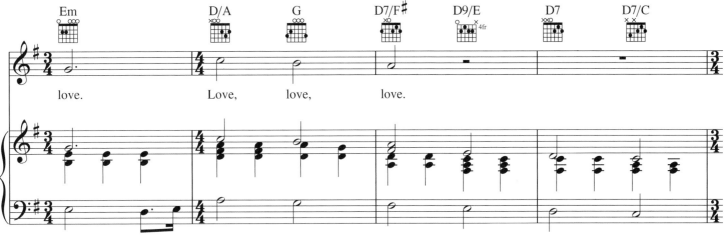

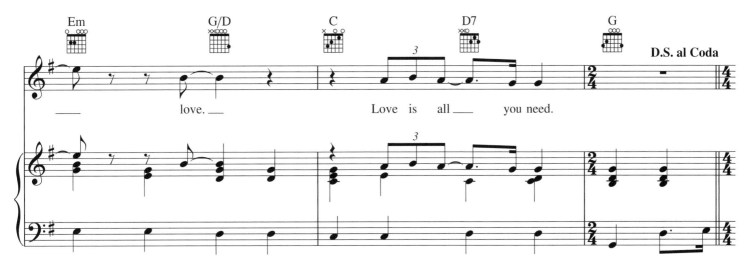

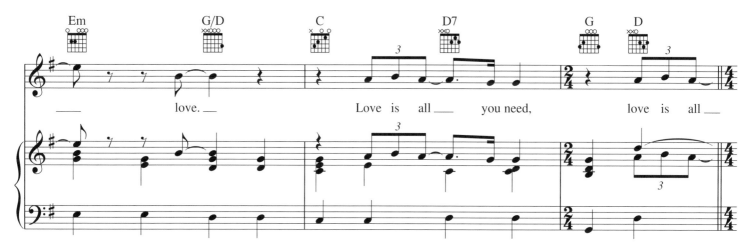

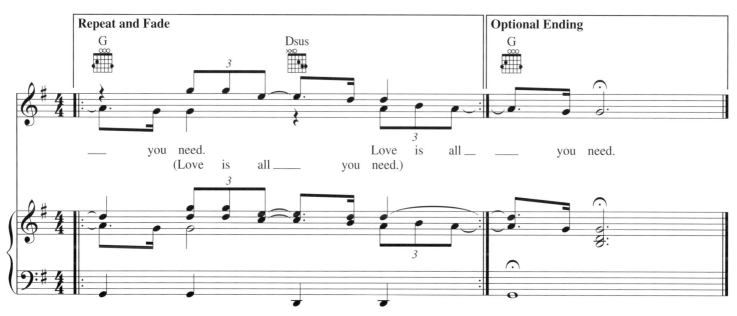

COME TOGETHER

Words and Music by JOHN LENNON
and PAUL McCARTNEY

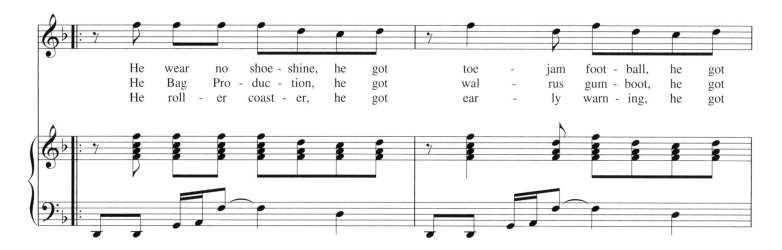

He wear no shoe-shine, he got toe - jam foot-ball, he got
He Bag Pro-duc-tion, he got wal - rus gum-boot, he got
He roll - er coast-er, he got ear - ly warn-ing, he got

mon - key fin-ger, he shoot Co - ca Co-la, he say, "I know_ you,
O - no side-board,he one spi - nal crack-er, he got feet down be-low_
mud - dy wa-ter, he one Mo - jo fil-ter, he say, "One and one and one_

you know me." _ One thing I can tell you is you got to be free. _
_ his knee. _ Hold you in his arm-chair, you can feel his dis - ease. _ } Come to-geth-
_ is three." _ Got to be good-look-ing 'cause he so hard to see. _

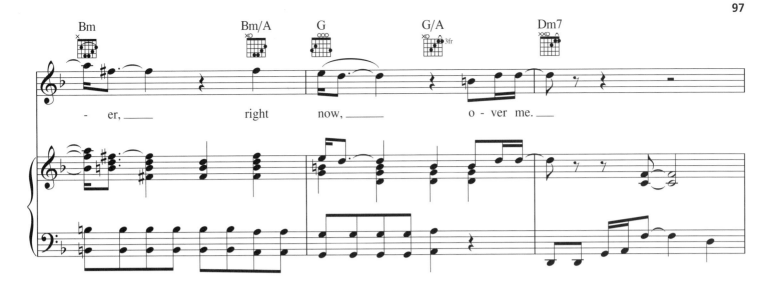

er, _____ right now, _____ o - ver me. _____

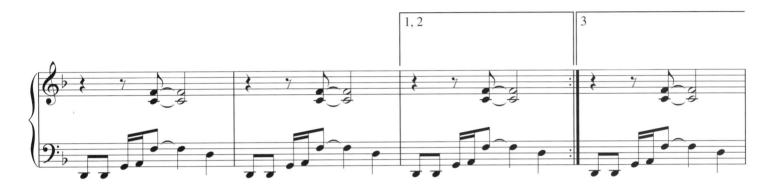

Repeat and Fade

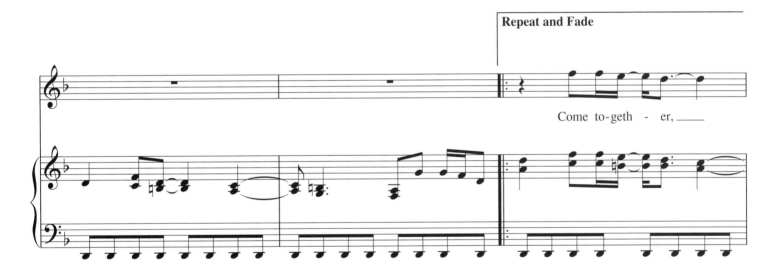

Come to-geth - er, _____

Optional Ending

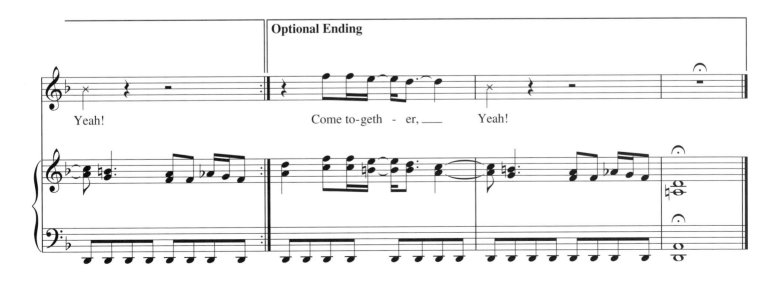

Yeah!   Come to-geth - er, _____ Yeah!

AMERICAN PIE

Words and Music by
DON McLEAN

A long, long time a-go I can still re-mem-ber how that

mu - sic used to make me smile. _____ And

I knew if I had my chance that I could make those peo - ple dance and

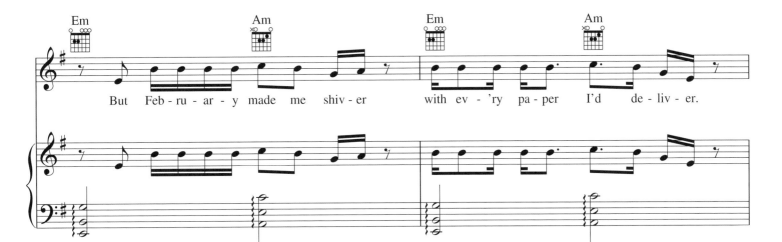

This - 'll be the day ___ that I ___ die. ___

{ 1. Did you ___ write the book of love ___ and do you ___
{ 2.-4. *(See additional lyrics)*

___ have faith in God a - bove? ___ If the Bi - ble tells ___

___ you so. ___ Now do you ___ be - lieve ___ in

rock and roll? __ Can mu - sic save your mor - tal soul __ and

can you teach me how to dance __ real slow? _____

_____ Well, I know that you're __ in love with him __ 'cause I _____

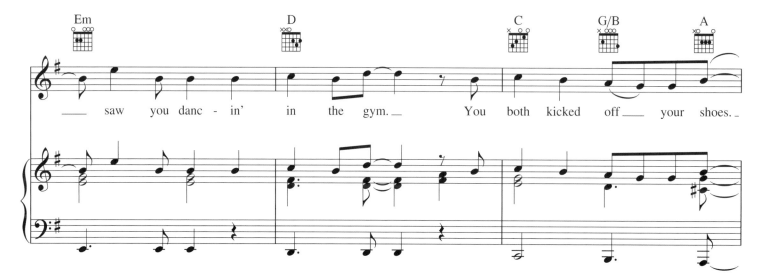

_____ saw you danc - in' in the gym. __ You both kicked off __ your shoes. __

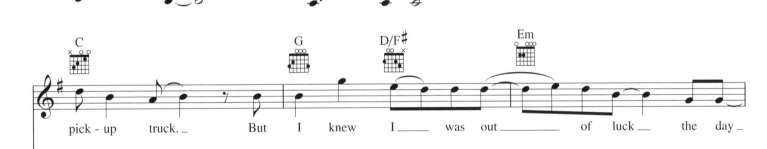

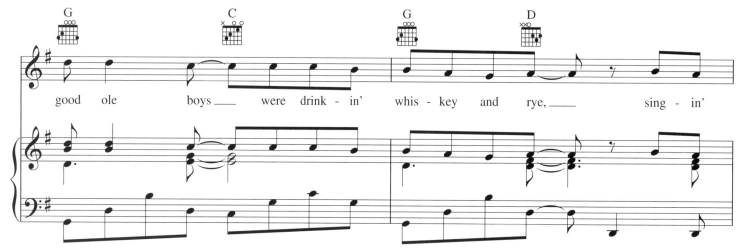

105

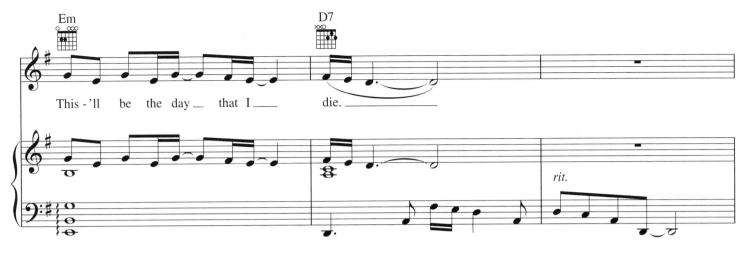

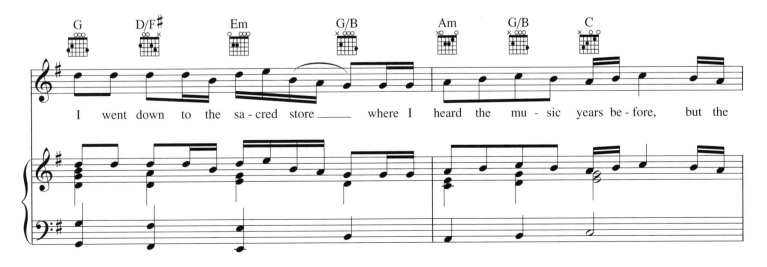

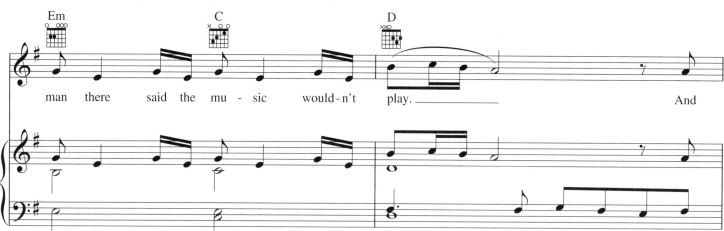

man there said the mu - sic would-n't play. _____ And

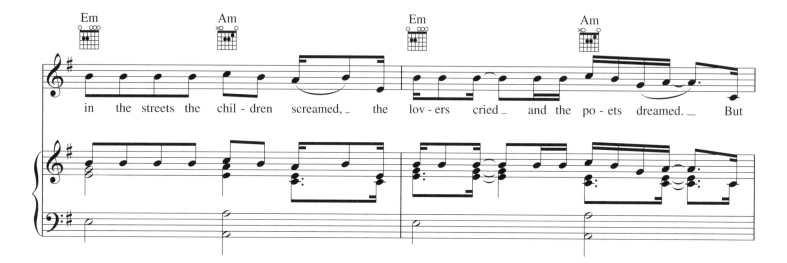

in the streets the chil - dren screamed, _ the lov - ers cried _ and the po - ets dreamed. _ But

not a word was spo - ken, the church bells all were bro - ken. And the three men I ad - mire most, the

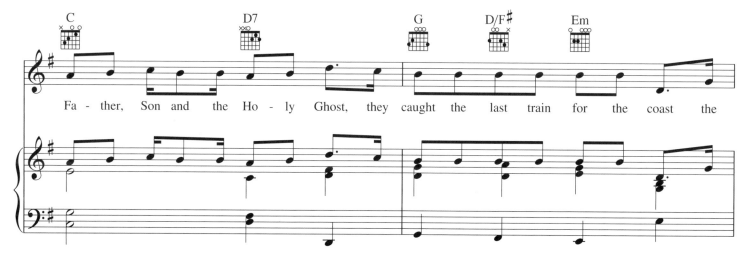

Fa - ther, Son and the Ho - ly Ghost, they caught the last train for the coast the

day the mu - sic died. And they were sing - in'

this - 'll be the day ___ that I ___ die. ___

Additional Lyrics

2. Now for ten years we've been on our own,
   And moss grows fat on a rollin' stone
   But that's not how it used to be
   When the jester sang for the king and queen
   In a coat he borrowed from James Dean
   And a voice that came from you and me
   Oh and while the king was looking down,
   The jester stole his thorny crown
   The courtroom was adjourned,
   No verdict was returned
   And while Lenin read a book on Marx
   The quartet practiced in the park
   And we sang dirges in the dark
   The day the music died
   We were singin'...bye-bye...etc.

3. Helter-skelter in the summer swelter
   The birds flew off with a fallout shelter
   Eight miles high and fallin' fast,
   It landed foul on the grass
   The players tried for a forward pass,
   With the jester on the sidelines in a cast
   Now the half-time air was sweet perfume
   While the sergeants played a marching tune
   We all got up to dance
   But we never got the chance
   'Cause the players tried to take the field,
   The marching band refused to yield
   Do you recall what was revealed
   The day the music died
   We started singin'... bye-bye...etc.

4. And there we were all in one place,
   A generation lost in space
   With no time left to start again
   So come on, Jack be nimble, Jack be quick,
   Jack Flash sat on a candlestick
   'Cause fire is the devil's only friend
   And as I watched him on the stage
   My hands were clenched in fits of rage
   No angel born in hell
   Could break that Satan's spell
   And as the flames climbed high into the night
   To light the sacrificial rite
   I saw Satan laughing with delight
   The day the music died
   He was singin'...bye-bye...etc.

FLY LIKE AN EAGLE

Words and Music by
STEVE MILLER

Tick, tock,_ tick. Doot, doot, do, do.

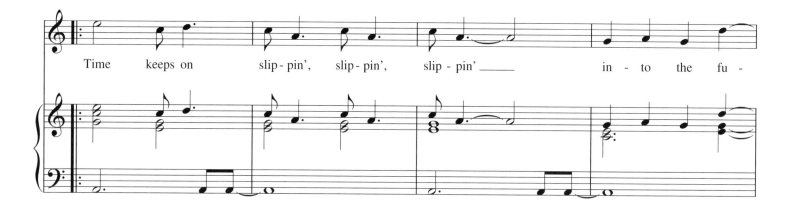

Time keeps on slip-pin', slip-pin', slip-pin' _____ in-to the fu-

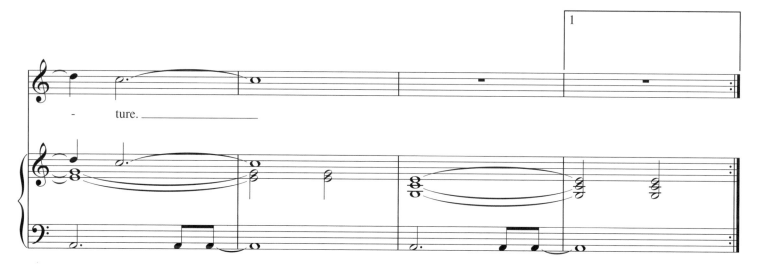

-ture. _____

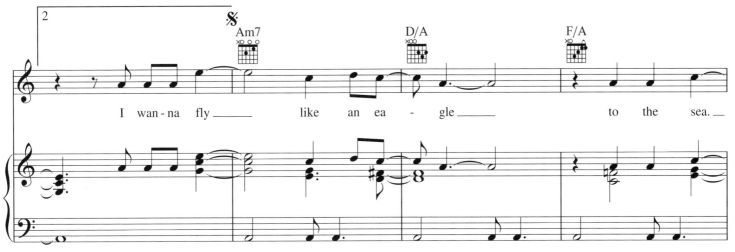

I wan-na fly ___ like an ea - gle ___ to the sea. __

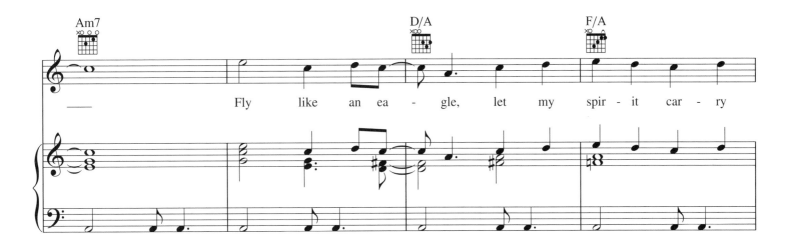

___ Fly like an ea - gle, let my spir - it car - ry

me. I want to fly like an ea - gle ___ { till I'm free. __
{ till I'm free, __

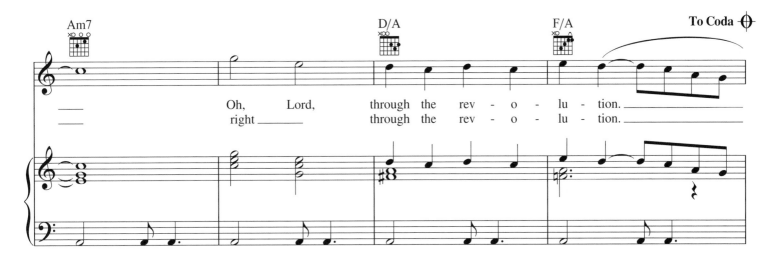

Oh, Lord, through the rev - o - lu - tion. ___
right ___ through the rev - o - lu - tion. ___

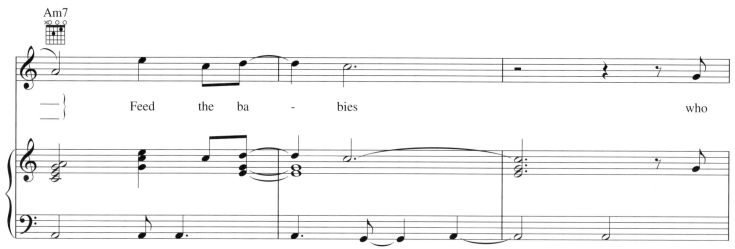

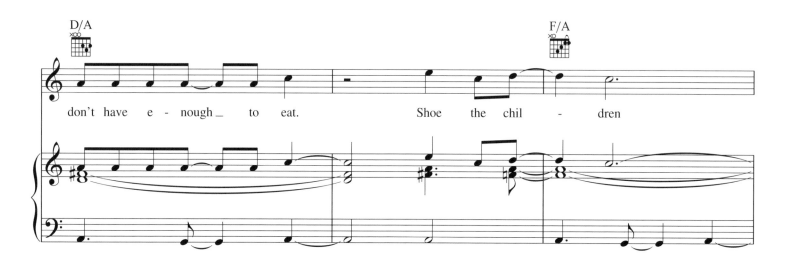

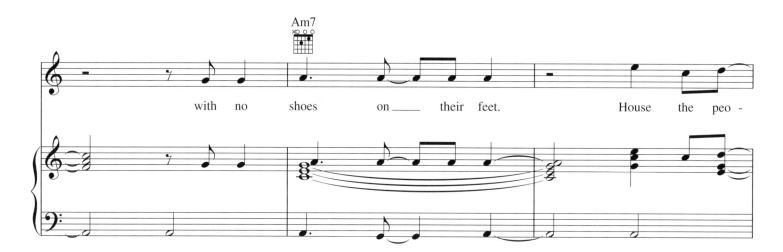

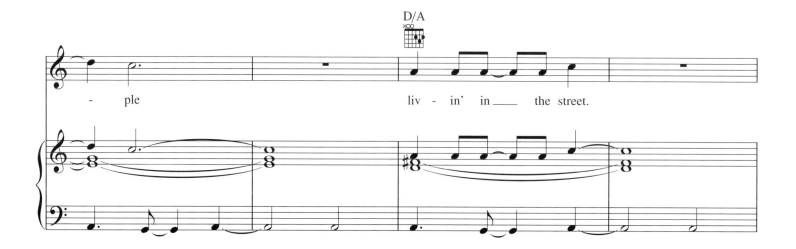

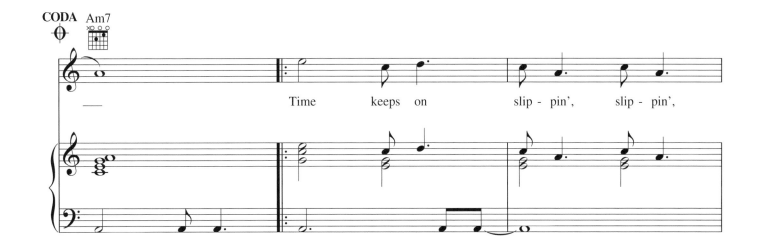

112

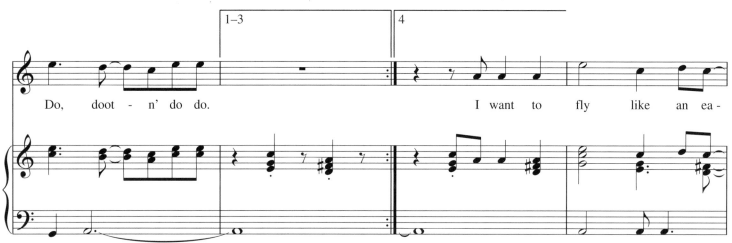

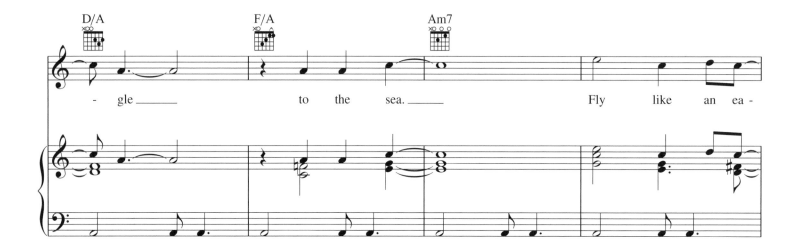

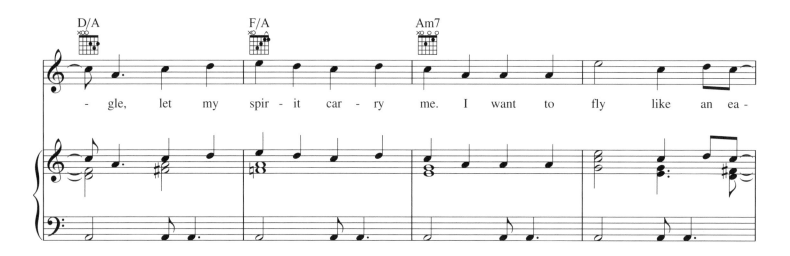

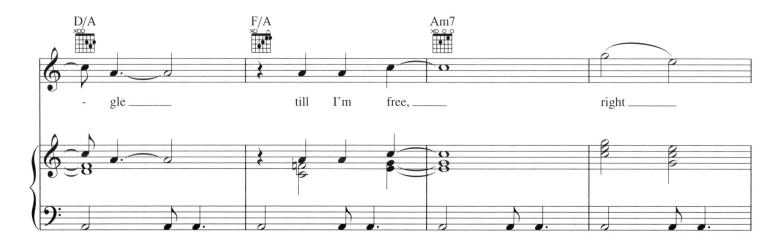

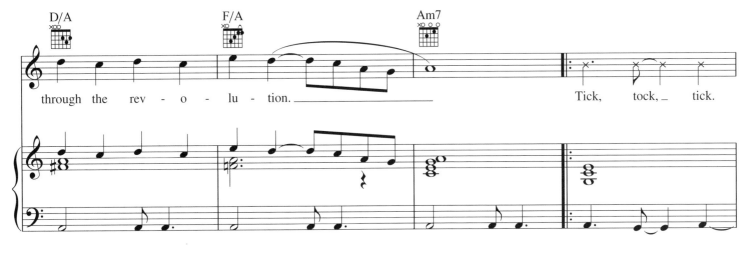

through the rev - o - lu - tion._____ Tick, tock,__ tick.

Doot, doot, do, do. Time keeps on

Play 4 times

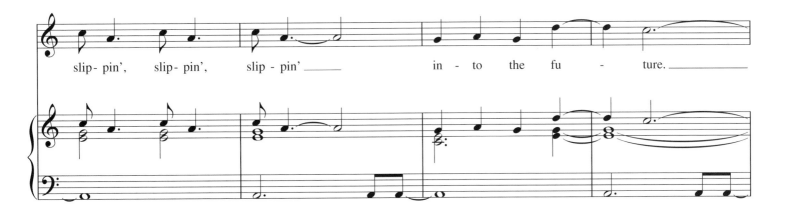

slip- pin', slip- pin', slip- pin'_____ in - to the fu - ture._____

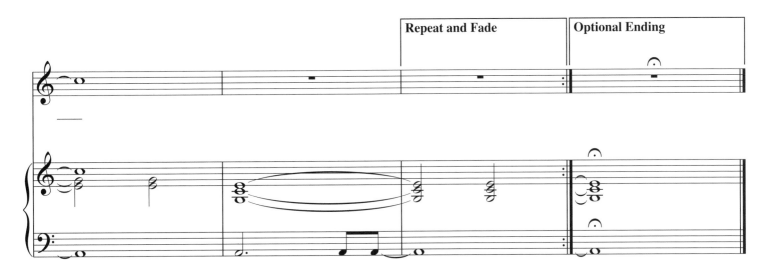

Repeat and Fade | **Optional Ending**

FROM A DISTANCE

Words and Music by
JULIE GOLD

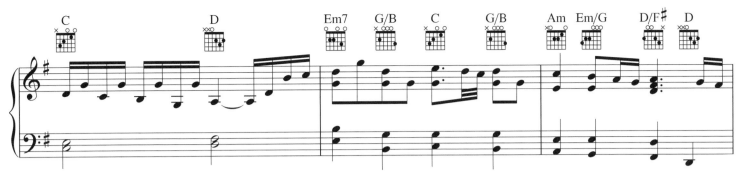

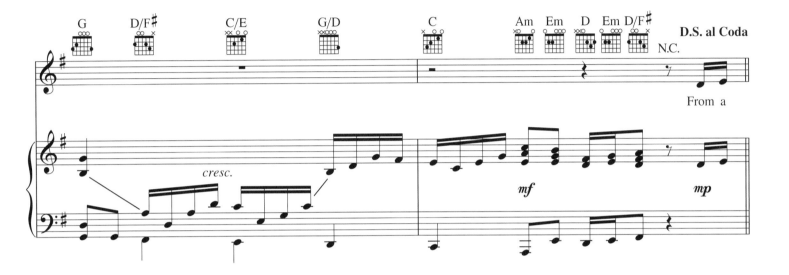

D.S. al Coda

From a

heart _____ of ev - 'ry ___ man. _____ It's the

hope of ___ hopes, _ it's the love of ___ loves. _ This is the song ___ of ___ ev - 'ry

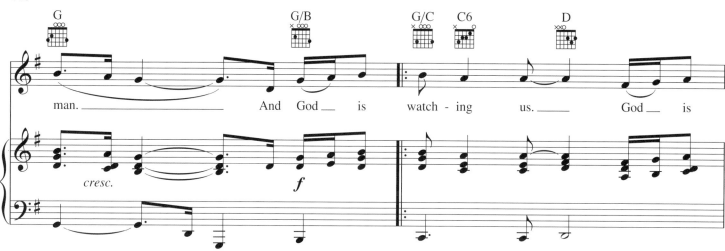

man. _____ And God __ is watch-ing us. ___ God __ is

watch-ing us. ___ God __ is watch-ing us _____ from a _____

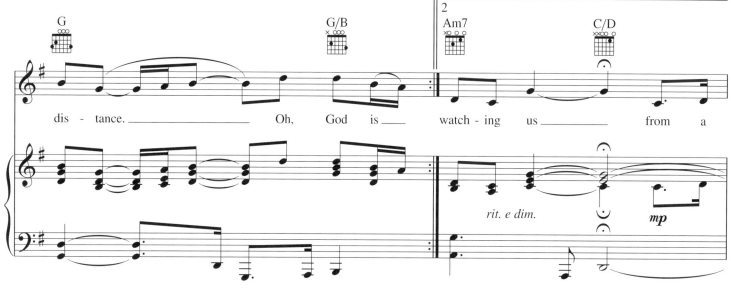

dis-tance. _____ Oh, God is ___ watch-ing us _____ from a

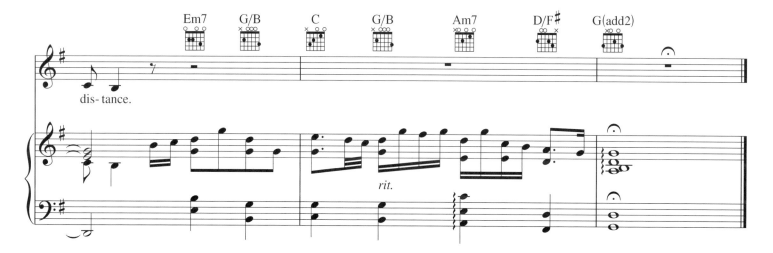

dis-tance.

SOMEWHERE OUT THERE
from AN AMERICAN TAIL

Music by BARRY MANN and JAMES HORNER
Lyric by CYNTHIA WEIL

Moderately, with expression

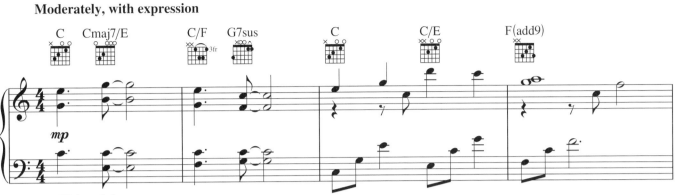

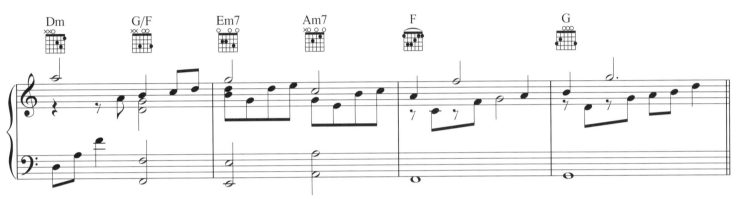

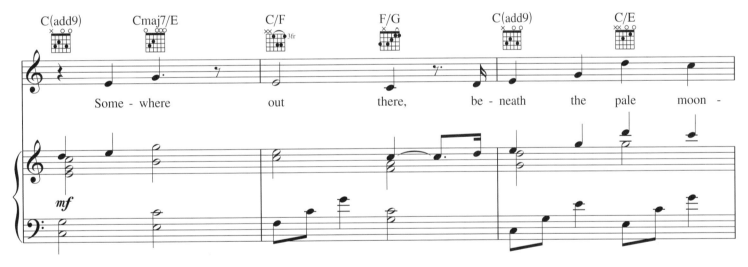

Some - where out there, be - neath the pale moon -

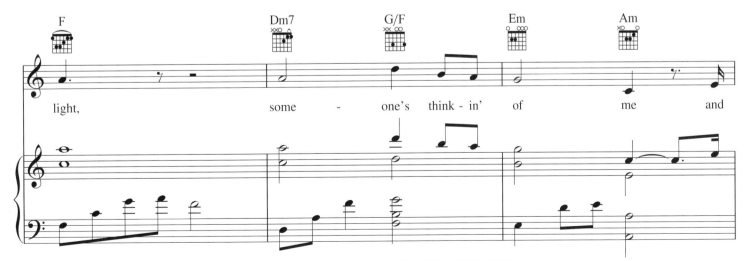

light, some - one's think - in' of me and

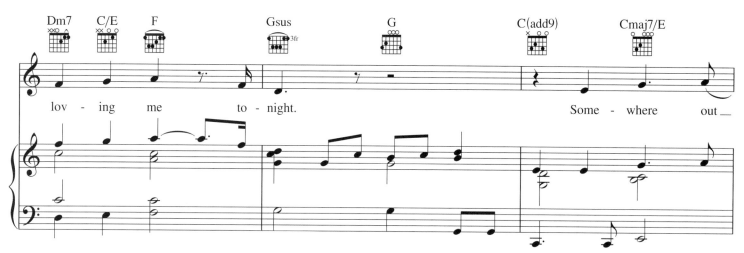

lov - ing me to - night. Some - where out __

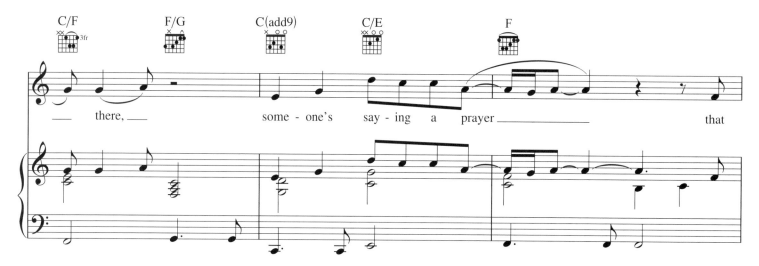

__ there, __ some - one's say - ing a prayer __ that

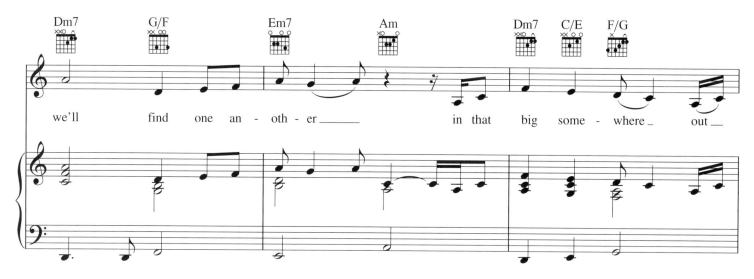

we'll find one an - oth - er __ in that big some - where __ out __

there. And e - ven though I know how ver - y far a - part __ we are __ it

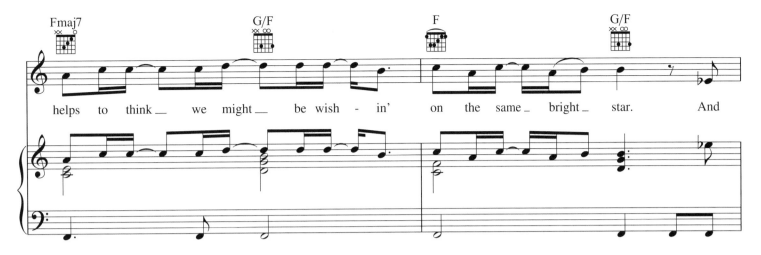

helps to think __ we might __ be wish - in' on the same __ bright __ star. And

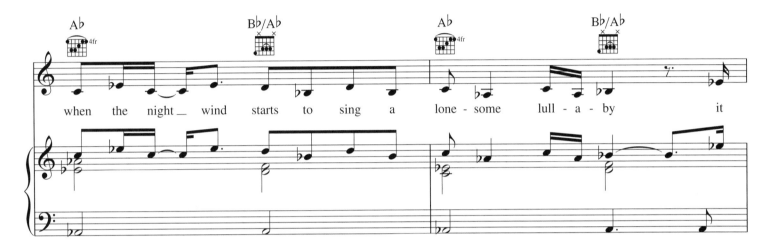

when the night __ wind starts to sing a lone - some lull - a - by it

helps to think we're sleep - ing un - der - neath the same big sky.

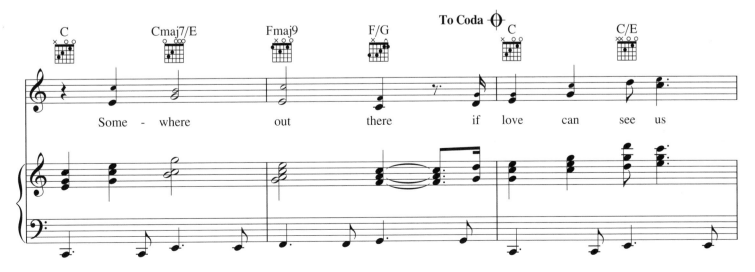

Some - where out there if love can see us

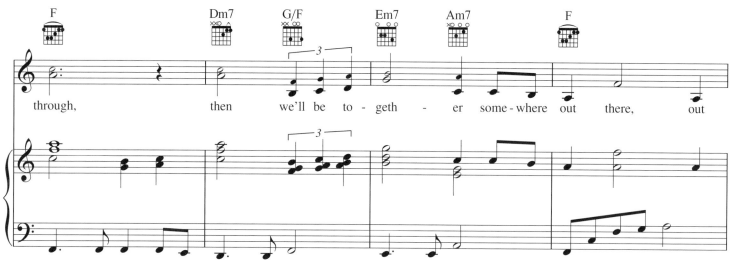

through, then we'll be to - geth - er some - where out there, out

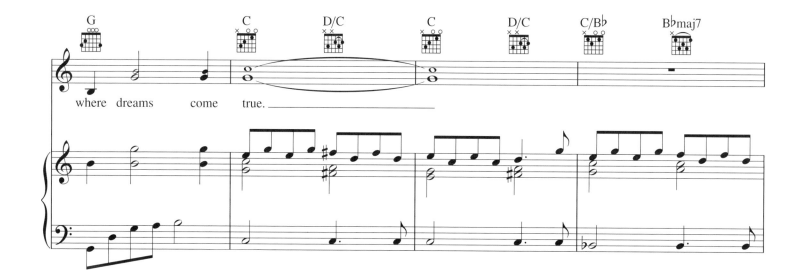

where dreams come true.

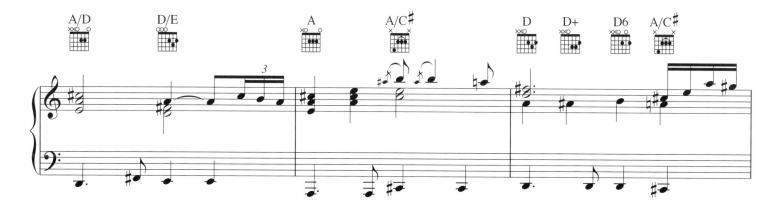

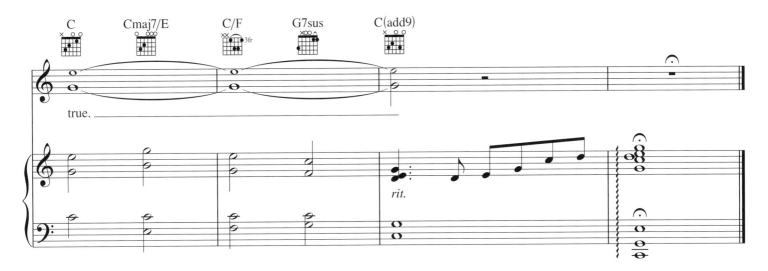

IMAGINE

Words and Music by
JOHN LENNON

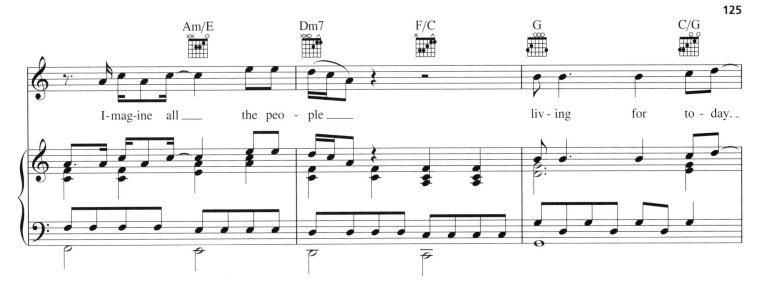

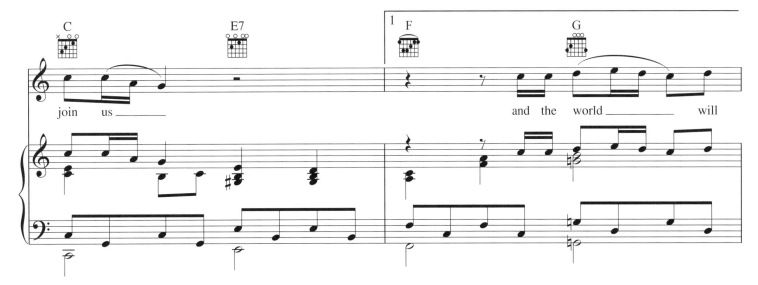

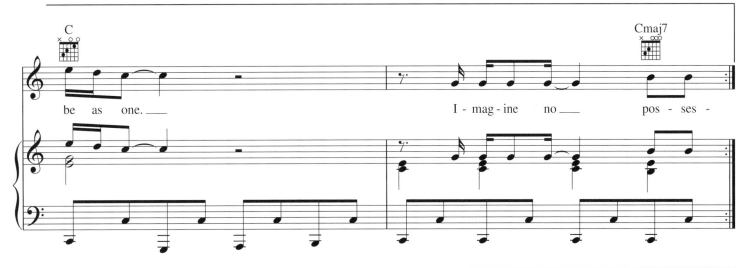

WE ARE FAMILY

Words and Music by NILE RODGERS
and BERNARD EDWARDS

(Yeah, yeah, yeah, ___ yeah, yeah, yeah.)

Ev - 'ry - one ___ can see ___ we're to - geth -

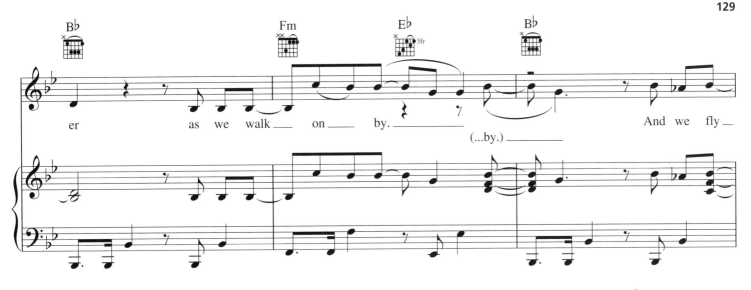

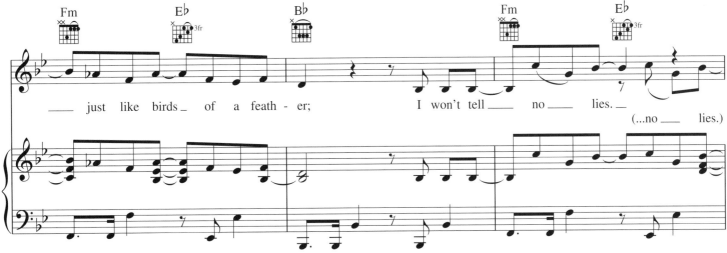

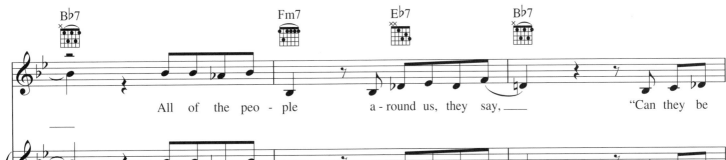

we're giv-ing love like a fam-'ly does, oh,___ yeah. We are fam-i-ly;

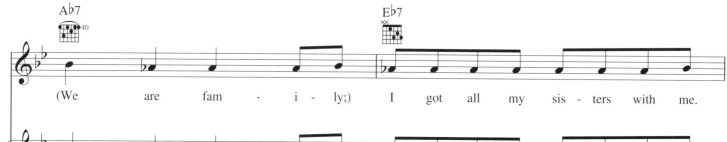

(We are fam-i-ly;) I got all my sis-ters with me.

(I got all my sis-ters with me.) We are fam-i-ly; (We are fam-i-ly.)

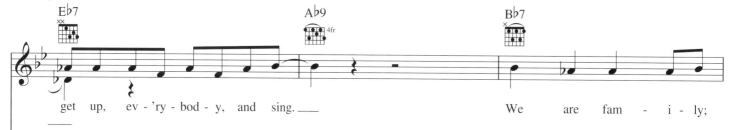

get up, ev-'ry-bod-y, and sing.___ We are fam-i-ly;

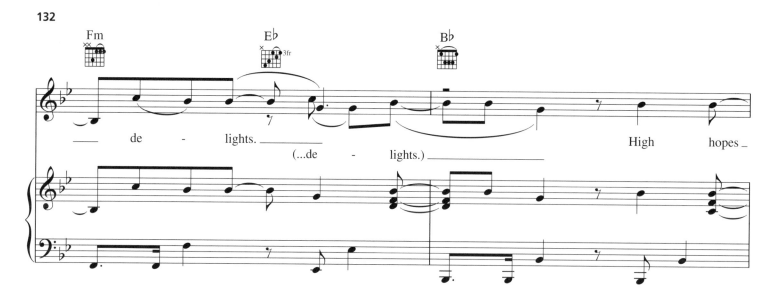

de - lights. _____ (...de - lights.) _____ High hopes _

_____ we _____ have _ for the fu - ture, and our goal's in sight. _____

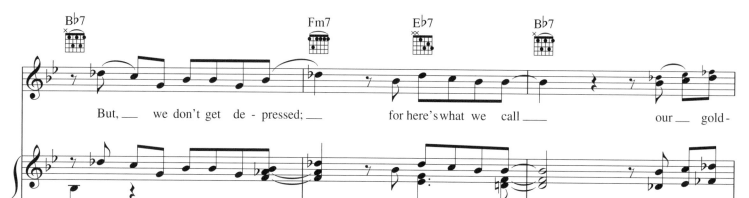

But, ___ we don't get de - pressed; ___ for here's what we call ____ our ___ gold-

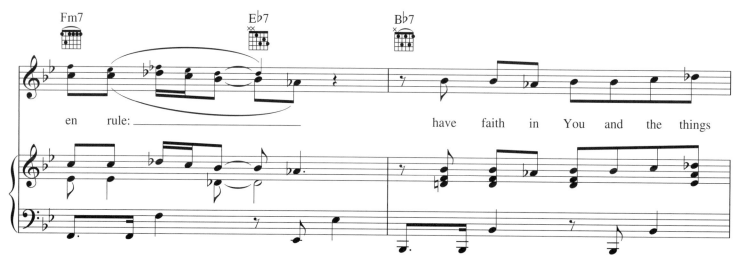

en rule: _____ have faith in You and the things

you do, you won't go wrong,_ oh no. This is our fam - 'ly jewel, yeah,_ yeah.___

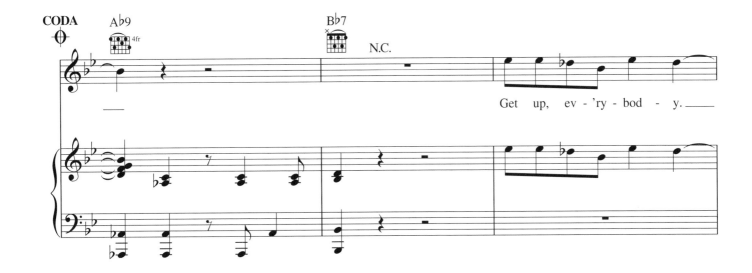

Get up, ev - 'ry - bod - y.___

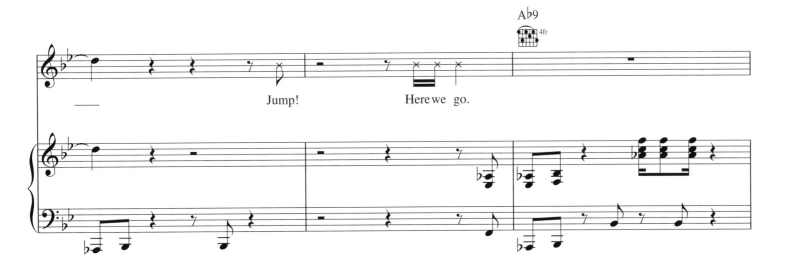

Jump! Here we go.

WE ARE THE WORLD

Words and Music by LIONEL RICHIE
and MICHAEL JACKSON

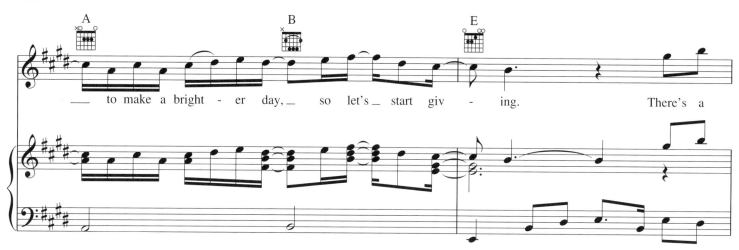

to make a bright - er day,_ so let's_ start giv - ing. There's a

choice we're mak - ing,_____ we're sav - ing our_ own lives,_ it's true;_

_____ we make_ bet - ter days,_ just you_ and me._

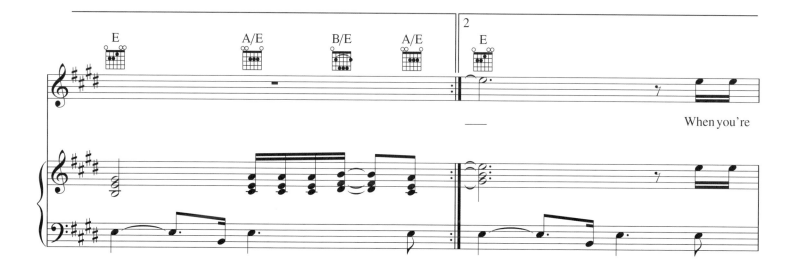

_____ When you're

139

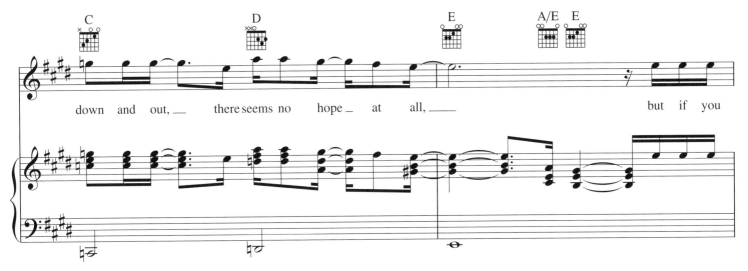

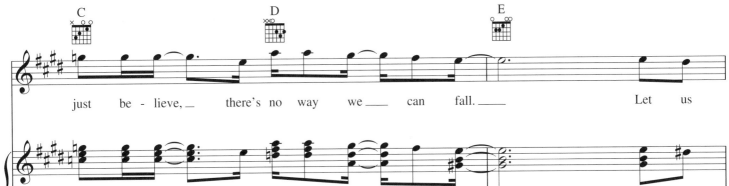

we are the chil - dren, we are the ones

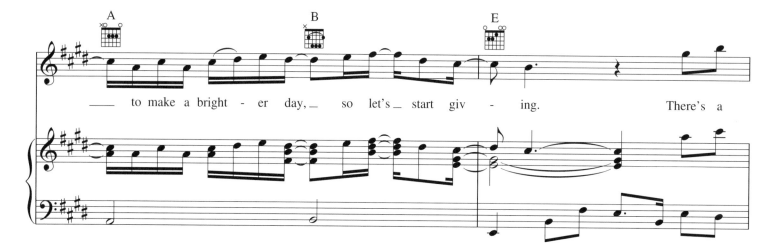

to make a bright - er day, _ so let's _ start giv - ing. There's a

choice we're mak - ing, _____ we're sav - ing our _ own lives, _ it's true; _

_ we make bet - ter days, just you _ and me. _ We are the world, _

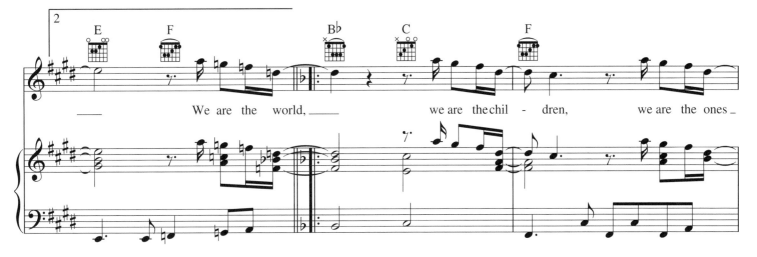

We are the world, _____ we are the chil - dren, we are the ones _

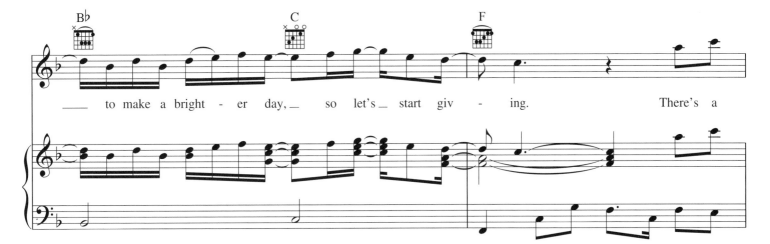

_____ to make a bright - er day, __ so let's __ start giv - ing. There's a

choice we're mak - ing, _____ we're sav - ing our __ own lives, _ it's true; _

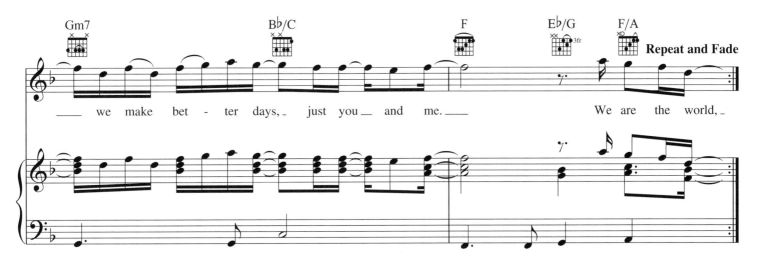

_____ we make bet - ter days, _ just you __ and me. __ We are the world, _

Repeat and Fade

WHAT A WONDERFUL WORLD

Words and Music by GEORGE DAVID WEISS
and BOB THIELE

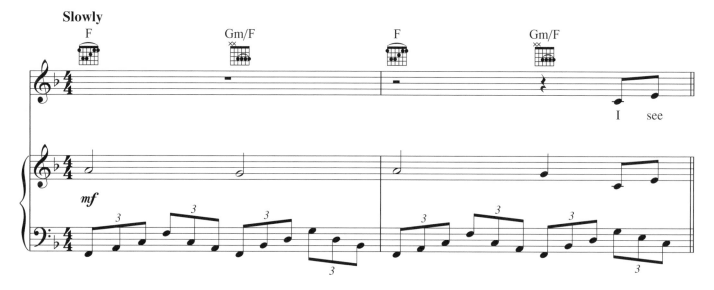

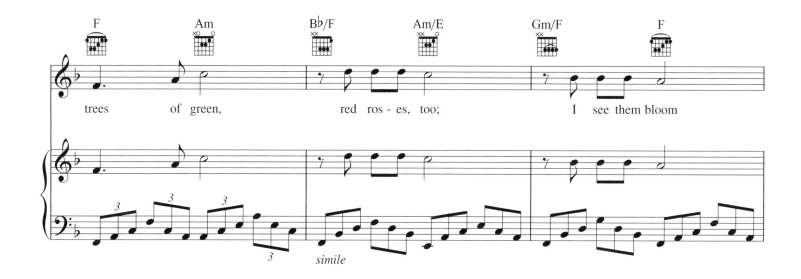

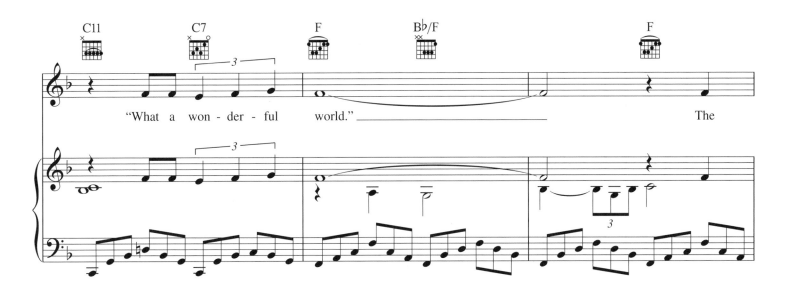

WHAT THE WORLD NEEDS NOW IS LOVE

Lyric by HAL DAVID
Music by BURT BACHARACH

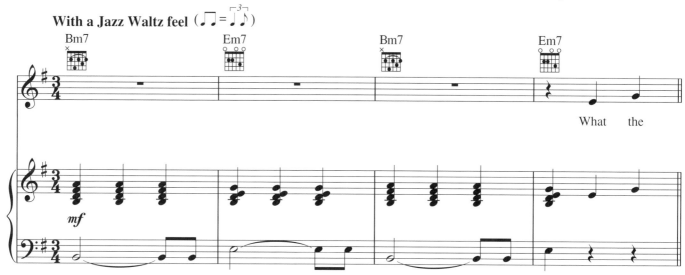

world needs now is love, sweet love.

It's the on-ly thing _____ that there's just _____ too lit-tle of. What the

world needs now is love, sweet love.

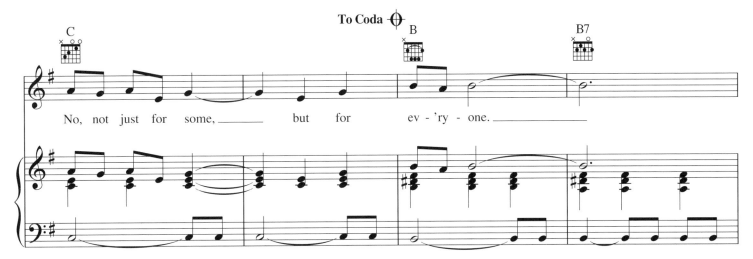

To Coda

No, not just for some, _____ but for ev - 'ry - one. _____

Lord, we don't need an - oth - er moun - tain. _____ There are
Lord, we don't need an - oth - er mead - ow. _____ There are

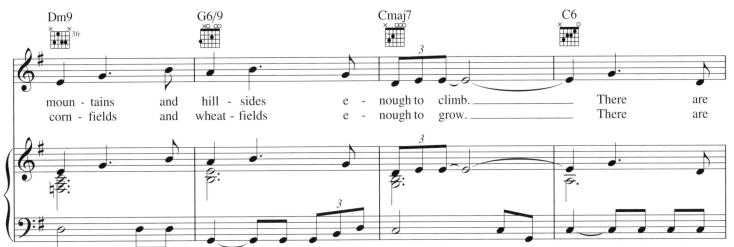

moun - tains and hill - sides e - nough to climb. _____ There are
corn - fields and wheat - fields e - nough to grow. _____ There are

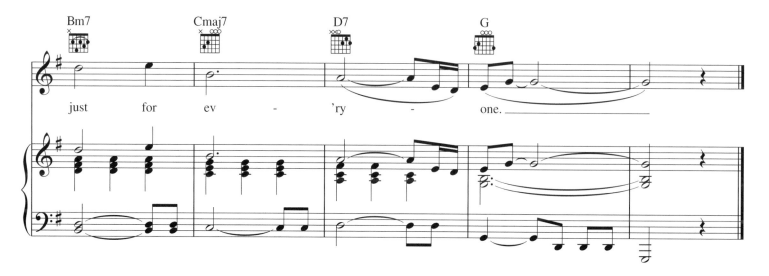

WOULDN'T IT BE NICE

Words by and Music by BRIAN WILSON,
TONY ASHER and MIKE LOVE

Shuffle

Would-n't it be nice if we were old-er, _ then _ we would-n't
nice if we could wake _ up _ in _ the morn-ing

have to wait _ so _ long _ and would-n't it be nice to live to-geth-
when the day _ is _ new _ and af-ter that to spend the day to-geth-

-er _ in _ the kind of world where we'd _ be - long. _
-er, _ hold each oth-er close the whole _ night _ through. _

might come __ true. _____
could - n't __ do. _____

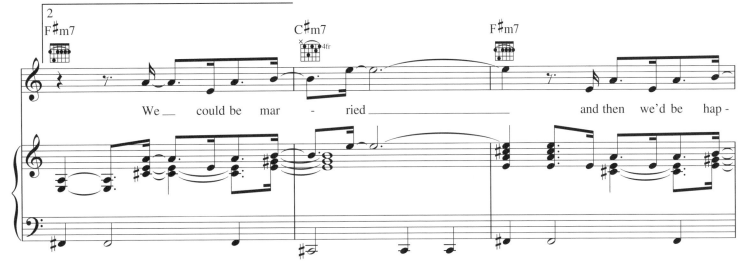

We __ could be mar - ried _____ and then we'd be hap -

- py. _____ Oh would-n't it __ be __ nice. _____

Optional Ending

Friendship

We all, at least occasionally, find ourselves down and in times of trouble,

in need of encouragement and support from those around us.

From Bill Wither's soulful classic "Lean on Me" to Daniel Powter's

relatively recent "Bad Day," these comforting and positive songs serve as

the perfect antidote to those dark moments.

Angel (page 164)

Released in 1997, "Angel" is the most well-known song by singer-songwriter Sarah McLachlan. Known for her mezzo-soprano voice and way with ballads, McLachan's "Angel" is quite haunting; it's about a struggle with chemical addiction, specifically that of the Smashing Pumpkins' touring keyboardist Jonathan Melvoin, who succumbed to a heroin overdose in 1996. Because "Angel" is such an intense number, it's been heard in emotional scenes on a number of television programs. And it is said the song has even saved a few lives, including that of rapper Darryl McDaniels (Run-D.M.C.).

Play "Angel," arranged here in C major, very gently and with as much emotion as you can muster. Feel free to add a bit of *rubato* — expressive slowing down or speeding up — to your playing. You might've noticed that McLachlan's original recording sounds a half step higher, in the key of D♭ major, than written here. *Transposing* — playing the same music in a different key — is an invaluable skill for a pianist to have, especially when accompanying a singer who requires a different key than what is written. So, once you've learned the song, if you're feeling adventurous, see if you can transpose it on sight. In the right hand of bar 1, for instance, instead of playing the chord E–G–C you'd play F–A♭–D♭.

Bad Day (page 157)

"Bad Day" was released in 2005 by the Canadian singer-songwriter Daniel Powter. The song was heard in a European Coca-Cola commercial before becoming the most successful single of 2006, according to *Billboard* magazine. The song even had a prominent role in the fifth installment of the wildly popular television show *American Idol*. In spite of all this, Powter failed to write any additional hits. But "Bad Day" continues to help listeners make light of those occasions when things aren't going their way.

"Bad Day" is written here in the somewhat difficult key of E♭ major. But what's most tricky about the song are its rhythms. There are plenty of syncopated 16th-note rhythms, so in learning the song, take things extremely slowly, subdividing throughout. Another thing to note is that whereas other songs in this collection have swung eighth notes, this one has swung *16th* notes. So, wherever you see a pair of consecutive 16ths, play and sing the first note longer than the second (at about a 2:1 ratio between the two notes). If this sounds confusing to you, just listen closely to the original recording of the song and try playing along with it.

Can't Smile Without You (page 170)

A singer-songwriter, producer, arranger, conductor, and more, Barry Manilow is a prodigiously talented musician. He's also one of the most popular entertainers of all time. In 1978, for instance, he had an amazing total of five albums charting simultaneously; no small feat. One of the songs that Manilow is most famous for is "Can't Smile Without You," which he released that same great year. The tune, supposedly inspired by the text on a greeting card, still serves Manilow well when he sings it in concert to several generations of fans.

When playing "Can't Smile Without You," in the key of G major, don't forget to swing those eighth notes throughout. This will really make the song come alive. Another thing to look out for is the song's numerous modulations. In bar 33 the music moves up a half step, to A♭ major, then up another half step, to A major in bar 49, before settling in yet another half step higher, to B♭ major in bar 57. The secret to smoothly navigating these modulations will be to learn each section separately before combining everything, and making sure not to drop the rhythm as you modulate.

Forever Young (page 176)

"Forever Young" is a Bob Dylan song that appeared in two versions on his 1974 album *Planet Waves*. The song subconsciously inspired singer-songwriter Rod Stewart's 1988 tune of the same name, and due to the similarities between the two versions Dylan now shares songwriting credits on Stewart's song. In any case, Stewart's version went all the way to #12 on the pop charts, and with its prayer-like lyrics it continues to provide listeners with inspiring words to live by.

Stewart recorded a mellower version of "Forever Young" in 1996, but this arrangement is based on the more driving 1988 version. Based in the key of E major, the music kicks off with an insistent single-note pattern in the left hand. If this part is too difficult, you can simply omit the 16th notes and instead play straight eighths, just like the left hand notation where the lyrics begin in bar 6. With its stripped-down texture, the right-hand part will be easy to play. If you encounter any difficulties, first learn the melody (up-stemmed notes) before adding the second layer (down-stemmed notes). Once you've put everything together, remember to play with a driving beat to make this song rock.

I Hope You Dance (page 190)

When the songwriter Tia Sillers wrote "I Hope You Dance," she was in the middle of a painful divorce. So, she escaped to the Florida Gulf Coast, where sitting on a beach she was able to gain some perspective on her troubles and reflect on her experiences in a positive way. This resulted in "I Hope You Dance," a song Sillers co-wrote with Mark D. Sanders, about being unafraid to step out and take chances in life. In 2000, the country singer Lee Ann Womack had a crossover hit with her recording of "I Hope You Dance." Womack's video for the song featured her tenderly singing the song to her own daughters.

"I Hope You Dance" is shown here in the key of G minor/B♭ major. Play it gently but not too slowly. Starting at the second ending is a type of notation, *divisi*, which might be new to you. The vocal clef includes parts for two different singers on the same staff. This section would be perfect to sing with a partner, but if you're on your own, just choose one of the parts to sing.

Lean on Me (page 198)

The great singer-songwriter Bill Withers was a latecomer to music; he didn't even record his first song until he was thirty-two years old. But having been in the U.S. Navy for nine years, Withers had plenty of rich life experiences from which to draw on in his songwriting. One of Withers' greatest songs is "Lean on Me," released in 1972. It has a soulful sound that evokes the rural South of Withers' youth. Yet, the lyrics, which encourage supportive and loving behavior among all people, reached out across geographic, cultural, and political lines, and "Lean on Me" became one of the greatest pop songs of all time.

"Lean on Me," arranged in C major, is perhaps not as complicated as it would appear in musical notation. The introduction (first eight bars) contains the bulk of the song's material. An interesting thing to note about the chords is that the notes travel straight up and down the C major scale (C–D–E–F–G–A–B). To better hear how this works, try playing the voices separately — start by playing the lowest note in each chord, then the middle, followed by the highest. One other thing to note: Throughout the piece, look out for the *8vb* signs (remember to play the music an octave lower than written) in the left-hand part.

Listen to Your Heart (page 183)

The Swedish pop duo Roxette — Marie Fredriksson and Per Gessle — enjoyed worldwide success in the late 1980s and early '90s. Around the time Roxette was most popular, the FM power ballad reigned supreme. So, the group responded to this trend by seeing just how huge of a ballad they could write. And what started off as a bit tongue-in-cheek ended up being one of Roxette's biggest hits, "Listen to Your Heart." While the original recording, with its slick production, might sound a little dated, this song can be great fun to play and sing unplugged, with piano and/or guitar.

"Listen to Your Heart" is arranged here in the slightly mournful key of A minor, modulating to D major/B minor, and then to C# minor. So, be sure that you can play each section cleanly before combining all three, and pay close attention to the transition between sections in order to modulate smoothly. Another thing to note is the song's use of suspended second (sus2) chords. For example, Asus2 includes the notes A, B, and E; Fsus2 includes F, G, and C. These chords have some close intervals — for example, in bar 3, the Fsus2 chord's F and G are a step a part, evoking a rather poignant sound.

Seasons of Love (page 206)

Rent, by Jonathan Larson, was one of the biggest new musicals of the 1990s. A rock opera, it is basically a retelling of Giacomo Puccini's *La Bohème*. The main differences: *Rent* is set in late-1980s New York instead of Paris, and features young artists struggling to survive in the shadow of AIDS as opposed to tuberculosis. "Seasons of Love" is one of the most popular numbers in *Rent*. The song, which addresses the passage of time, is sung by the entire cast at the beginning of the second act; on the original soundtrack is a wonderful alternate version with the R&B great Stevie Wonder.

Kicking off here in the key of F major, "Rent" has a fairly simple structure: The first four bars introduce an *ostinato*, or repeated figure, over which most of the lyrics are sung. So, in learning the song, make sure that you have the ostinato down cold before proceeding to the verse, and everything should fall smoothly into place. In bars 2 and 4, cleanly articulate the dotted-eighth to 16th note rhythm, which is crucial to achieving the song's rock feel. And in bar 21, while the music may appear completely different, the four-bar ostinato is basically just transposed up a fourth. So, if you learned the first section thoroughly, this one should be a breeze and you'll have the whole song mastered.

Stand by Me (page 211)

Ben E. King originally wrote "Stand by Me" for his R&B vocal group the Drifters. They passed on it, though, and it wasn't until King needed some extra material for a solo session that he pulled out the song again. So, one of the greatest songs in pop history was almost never recorded! In any case, King's 1960 original version has inspired some great covers, by the likes of John Lennon, U2, and even Cassius Clay (Muhammad Ali).

"Stand by Me," arranged in F major, is easy to read. When you run through the bass part, keep in mind the sound of an upright bass, and for the proper groove, be sure to heed the rests on beat 2. If the basic chord progression sounds familiar, that's because it's among the most common in all of pop music: I–vi–IV–V (F–Dm–B♭–C). Each chord is numbered by its position in the F major scale (F–G–A–B♭–C–D–E); uppercase numerals represent major chords and lowercase represent minor chords. For fun, see if you can find the same progression, perhaps in different keys, in other pop songs.

A Thousand Miles (page 214)

The young American singer-songwriter-pianist Vanessa Carlton is best known for her 2002 song "A Thousand Miles." The piece started off as a piano riff that Carlton wrote at her parents' house in 1998. She developed writer's block, but several months later the rest of the song came together in an hour for her. A few years after that, once Carlton had secured a record deal, the song was finally recorded with a lovely arrangement driven by piano and strings. And with its universal lyrics, dealing with yearning for something that has been lost, it resonated with listeners throughout the world, becoming one of the biggest songs of 2002.

"A Thousand Miles" has been arranged here in B♭ major, an easier key than that in which the song was originally recorded, B major. Of course, if you'd like to play the song in the original key, this would offer you a good opportunity to work on transposing. Whichever key you choose, the song is pretty rhythmically involved, with lots of 16th-note syncopations, so remember to take things slowly if needed. In the left hand, be especially mindful of the rests — remember, the rests that you don't play are as important as the notes you do.

You Raise Me Up (page 222)

The song "You Raise Me Up" was originally an instrumental piece, "Silent Story," composed by the Norwegian pianist Rolf Løvland of the piano-violin duo Secret Garden. Its melody was based on an old Irish tune, "Londonderry Air," more commonly known as "Danny Boy." Løvland asked Irish novelist Brendan Graham to add lyrics after reading Graham's *The Whitest Flower*, and the song finally became a hit when the singer Josh Groban recorded it in 2004. Testament to the greatness of "You Raise Me Up" is that in its short lifetime, it's already been covered more than 125 times by artists from all around the world.

When learning a new song that's based on, or inspired by an old one, it's always a good idea to check out the source material. So, before you learn how to play "You Raise Me Up," listen to a few recordings of "Danny Boy" if you're not already familiar with that tune. You might also seek out a few different interpretations of "You Raise Me Up." Once you've done all that, play the song, which starts off here in the key of E♭ major, slowly and with lots of expressiveness. *Crescendo* (gradually get louder) as the melody ascends and *decrescendo* when the melody descends, musically shaping the phrases of this lovely and inspiring ballad.

You'll Be in My Heart (Pop Version) (page 234)

In 1999, the English singer-songwriter-drummer Phil Collins had one of his biggest hits to date with "You'll Be in My Heart," featured in the Disney motion picture *Tarzan*.™ This tender song, for which Collins won an Oscar® award (Best Original Song), was heard in the film when Tarzan's adoptive mother sang to her orphaned son out of the need to protect him. Now more than a decade later, "You'll Be in My Heart" continues to warm the hearts of listeners throughout the world.

Tarzan featured two versions of "You'll Be in My Heart," the first sung by Glenn Close, who played the character of Tarzan's mother, and the second, a pop version, by Collins. Arranged here is the pop version, which kicks off in the difficult key of F# major — six sharps! The song modulates to a number of other keys, E♭ major, A♭ major in the second bar of the coda, and finally, F major just after the coda's second ending. So, as with all the other songs in this book, take things very slowly in learning each section before putting them together. Once you're comfortable with the key changes, play moderately but with a driving beat.

You've Got a Friend (page 228)

In 1971, the singer-songwriter Carole King released the song "You've Got a Friend" on her album *Tapestry*. While the album was a breakthrough for King and a huge influence on singer-songwriters of the 1970s, the song wasn't a hit for her. It was, however, a major hit that same year for King's friend James Taylor; around the same time it was also popular as a duet between the R&B singers Roberta Flack and Donnie Hathaway. The song has been covered extensively in the four decades since, by everyone from jazz singer Ella Fitzgerald to soul singer Al Green.

"You've Got a Friend" is arranged here in the bright key of A major. The piano part is fairly straightforward, however, there is one detail that might be a little confusing. In the bass clef of bar 5 and elsewhere you'll find the same note written in two different values on the same beat. Don't actually play the note twice; just hold it throughout the measure, as indicated by the whole note. The purpose of having the F# represented simultaneously as an eighth note and a whole note is to show that the same note is part of two different layers (or voices), both a bass note and another moving harmony line.

BAD DAY

Words and Music by
DANIEL POWTER

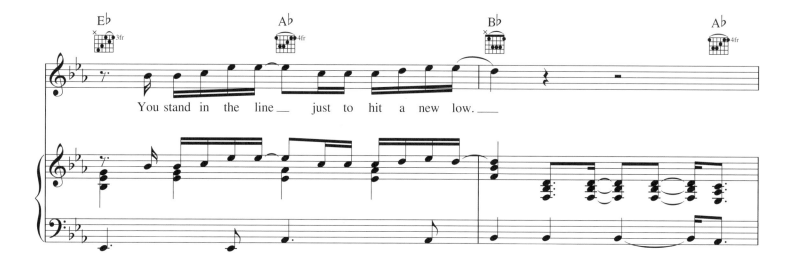

and I don't need no car-ryin' on be-cause you had a bad

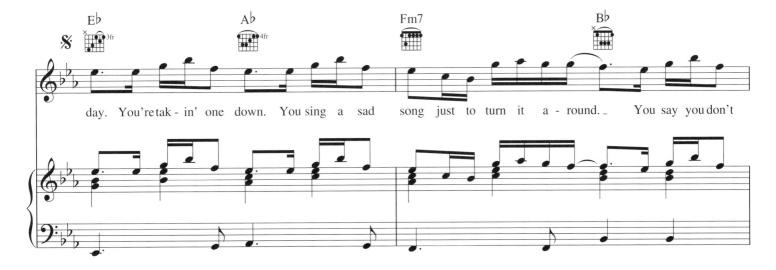

day. You're tak-in' one down. You sing a sad song just to turn it a-round. You say you don't

know. You tell me don't lie. You work at a smile and you go for a ride. You had a bad

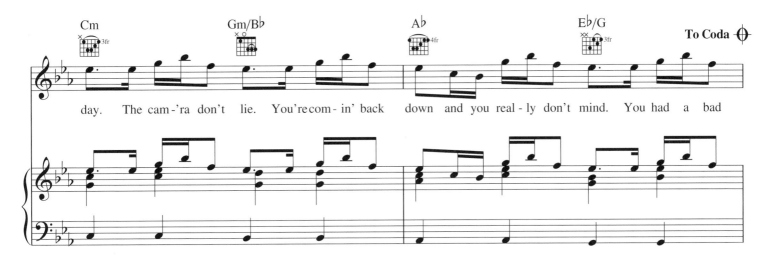

day. The cam-'ra don't lie. You're com-in' back down and you real-ly don't mind. You had a bad

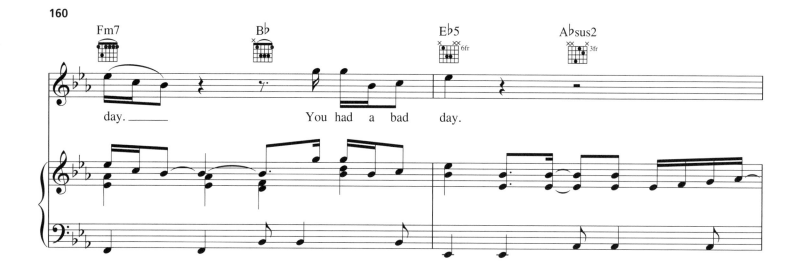

day. _____ You had a bad day.

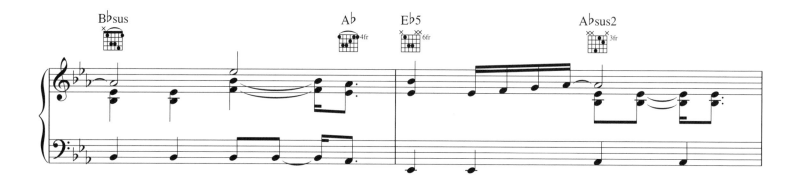

Well, you need a blue _ sky hol - i - day. _

_____ The point is they laugh _ at what _ you say ___ and I don't need _ no car - ryin' on. _

So where is the pas - sion when you need it the most?_

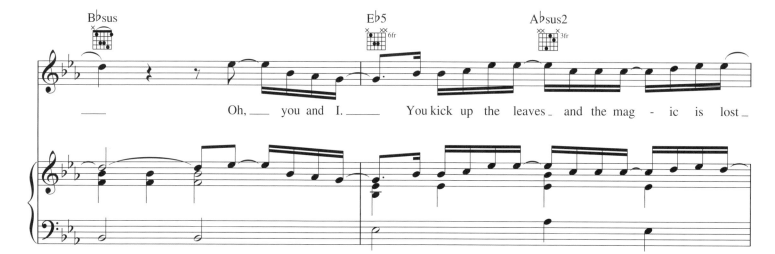

_ Oh, ___ you and I. _____ You kick up the leaves _ and the mag - ic is lost _

_ 'cause you had a bad day. You're tak - in' one down. You sing a sad

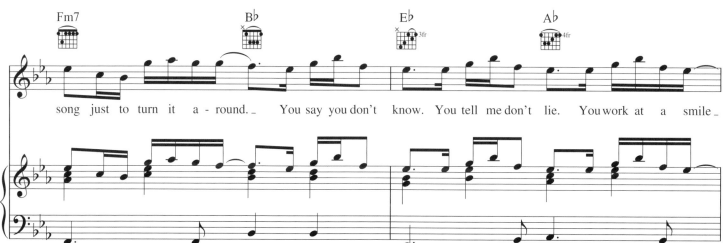

song just to turn it a - round. _ You say you don't know. You tell me don't lie. You work at a smile _

and you go for a ride.__ You had a bad day. You've seen what you like.__ And how does it feel__

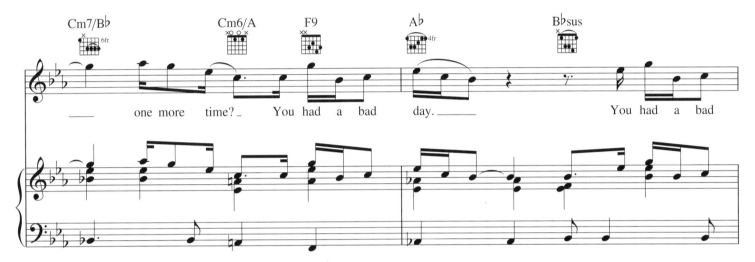

__ one more time?__ You had a bad day._____ You had a bad

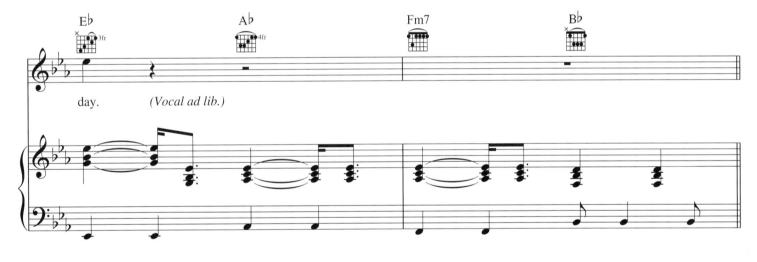

day. (Vocal ad lib.)

Repeat and Fade

(Vocal ad lib. continues)

Optional Ending

ANGEL

Words and Music by
SARAH McLACHLAN

*Recorded a half step higher.

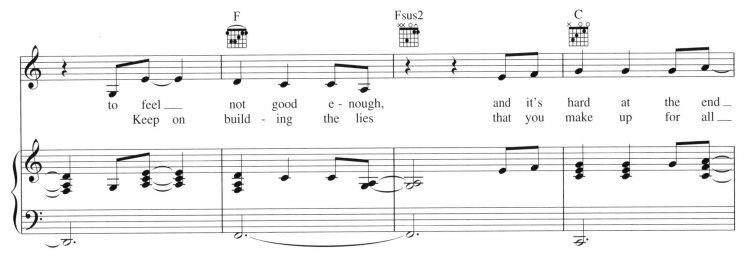

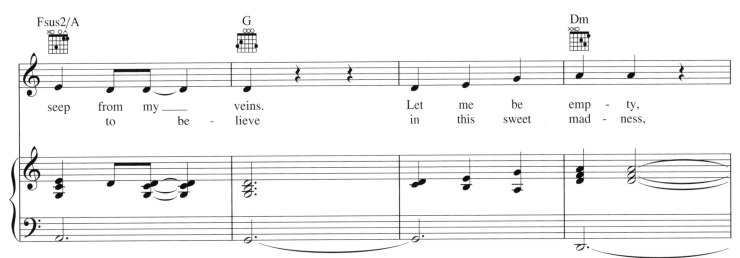

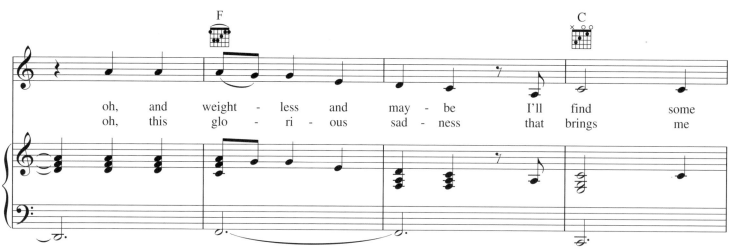

oh, and weight- less and may - be I'll find some
oh, this glo - ri - ous sad - ness that brings me

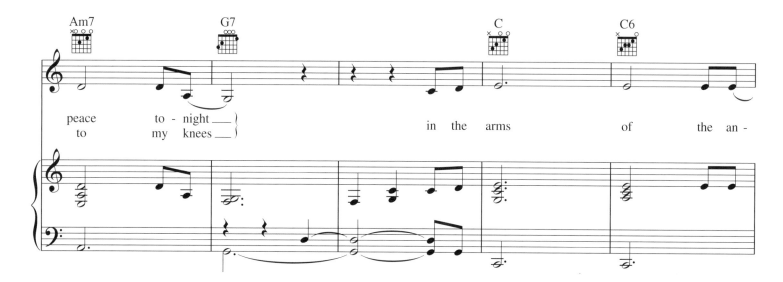

peace to - night ___ in the arms of the an -
to my knees ___

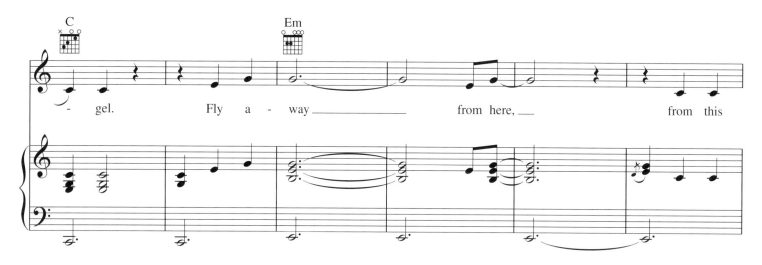

- gel. Fly a - way _____ from here, ___ from this

dark, cold _____ ho - tel room and ___ the end -

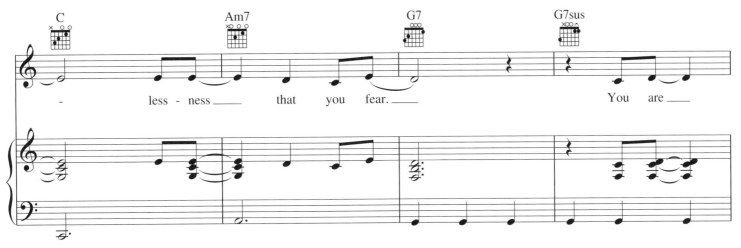

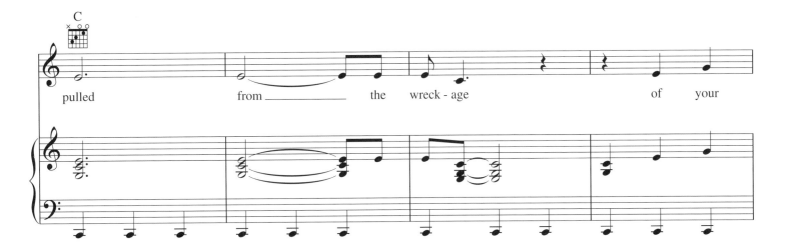

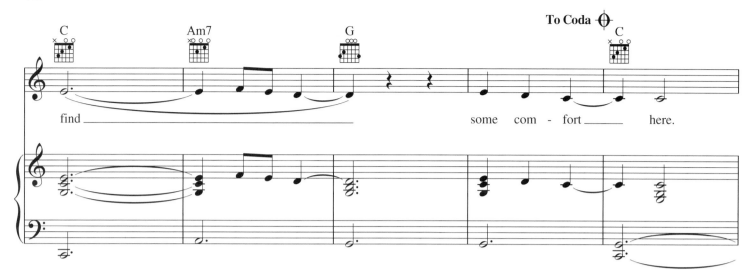

find _____ some com - fort ____ here.

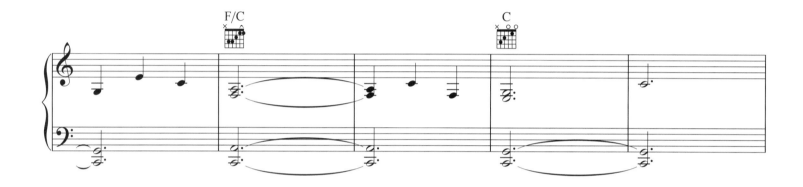

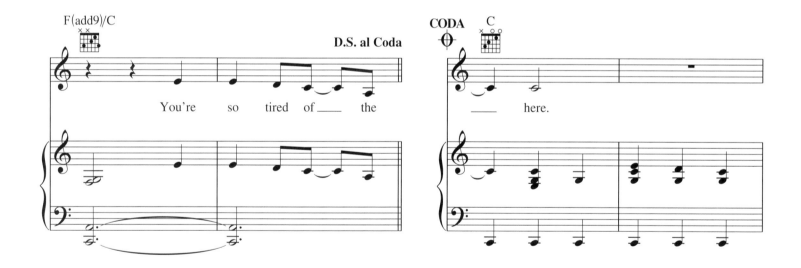

You're so tired of ___ the ____ here.

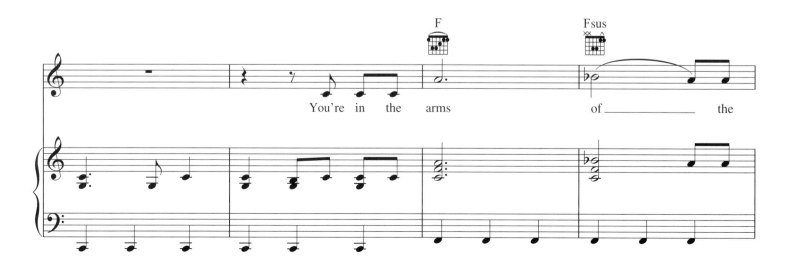

You're in the arms of _____ the

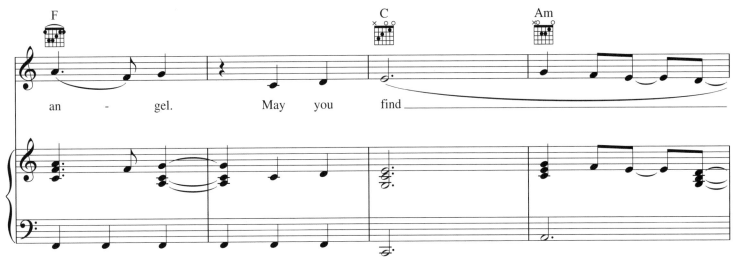

an - gel. May you find

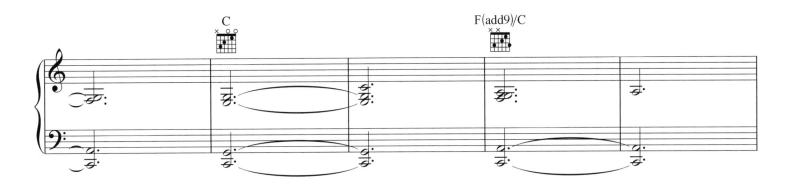

some com - fort _____ here. _____

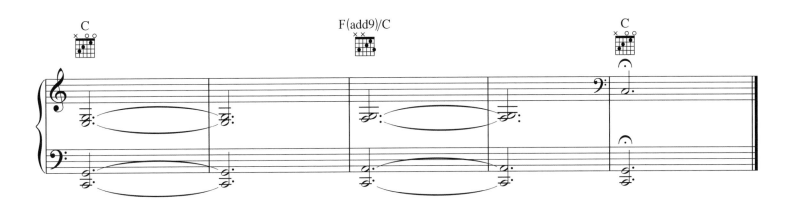

CAN'T SMILE WITHOUT YOU

Words and Music by CHRIS ARNOLD,
DAVID MARTIN and GEOFF MORROW

Lyrics:

You know I can't smile with-out you.
I feel sad when you're sad.
I can't smile with-out you.
I feel glad when you're glad.
I can't laugh and I can't sing. I'm find-in' it hard to do an-y-thing. You see, I
If you on-ly knew what I'm go-in' through.

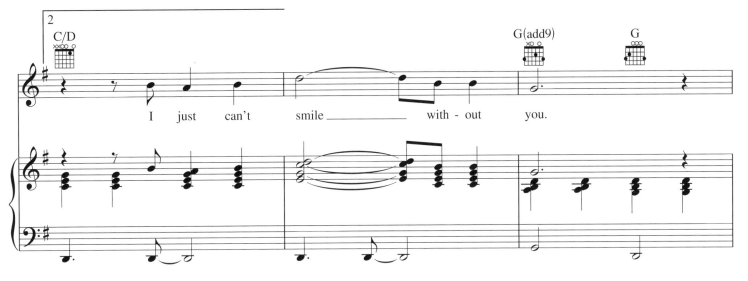

I just can't smile _____ with - out you.

You came a - long ___ just like a song, ___ and

bright-ened my day. ___ Who'd-'ve be-lieved that you were part of a dream? _

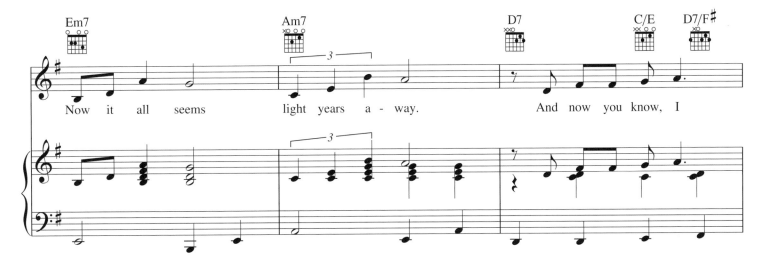

Now it all seems light years a - way. And now you know, I

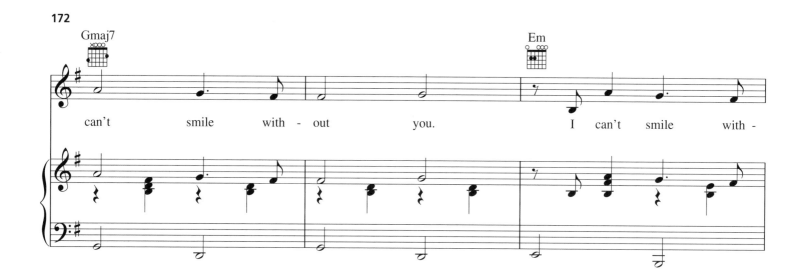

can't smile with - out you. I can't smile with -

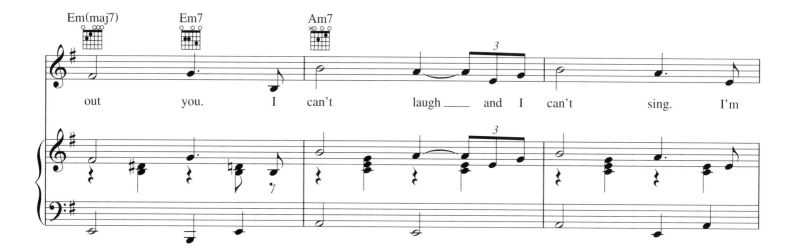

out you. I can't laugh___ and I can't sing. I'm

find - in' it hard___ to do an - y - thing.___ You see, I feel sad when

you're sad. I feel glad when you're___ glad. If

you ___ on - ly knew what I'm ___ go - ing through. I just can't

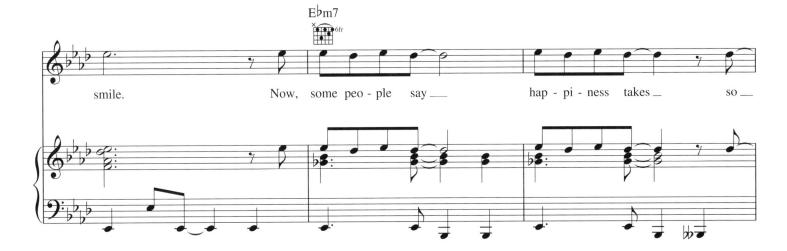

smile. Now, some peo - ple say ___ hap - pi - ness takes ___ so ___

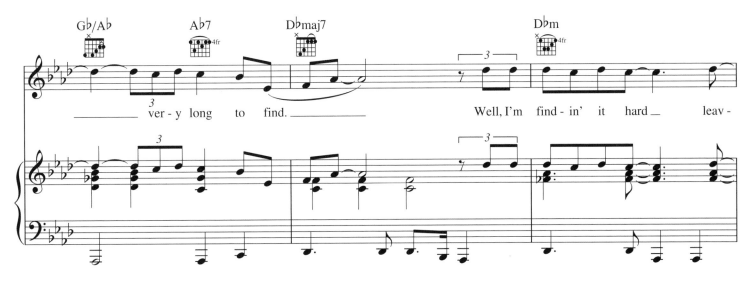

___ ver - y long to find. ___ Well, I'm find - in' it hard ___ leav -

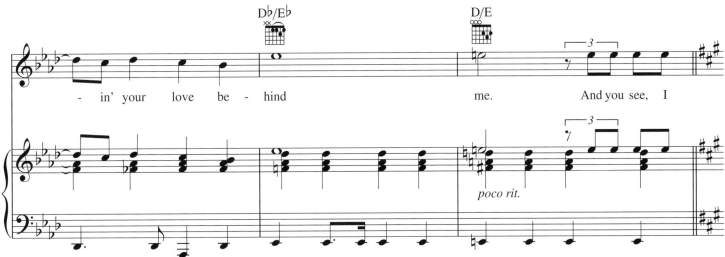

- in' your love be - hind me. And you see, I

poco rit.

FOREVER YOUNG

Words and Music by ROD STEWART,
KEVIN SAVIGAR, JIM CREGAN
and BOB DYLAN

Driving beat

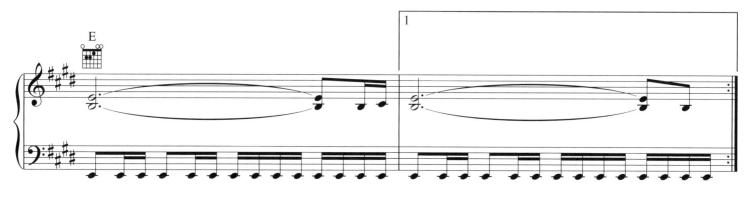

May the good Lord be with you down ev-er-y road you roam.

And may sun-shine and hap-pi-ness sur-

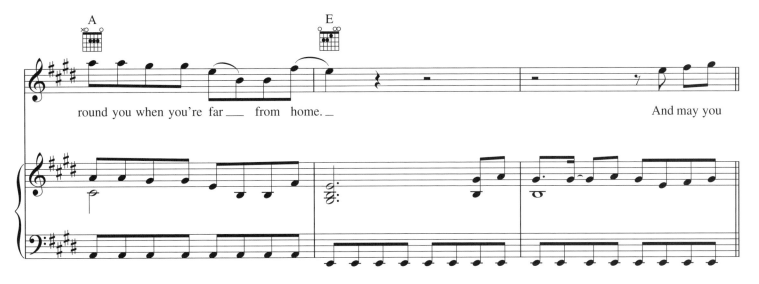

round you when you're far ___ from home. ___ And may you

grow ___ to be proud, ___ dig - ni - fied ___ and true. ___
for - tune be with you, may your guid - ing light ___ be strong, _
fi - n'lly fly a - way, I'll be hop - ing that I served ___ you well. ___

___ And do un - to oth - ers as
___ build a stair - way to heav-en with a
___ For all the wis - dom of a life - time,

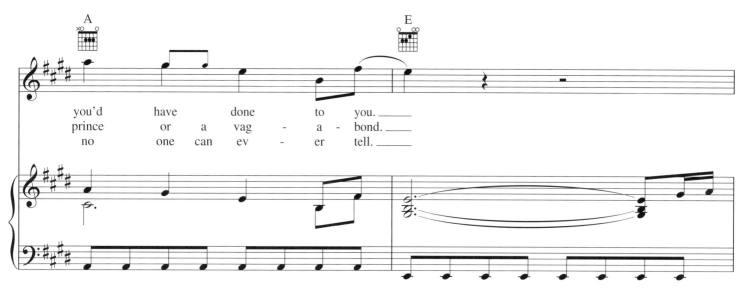

you'd   have   done   to   you. ____
prince   or   a   vag - a - bond. ____
no   one   can   ev - er   tell. ____

Be   cou - ra - geous   and ____ be   brave. ____
And   may   you   nev - er   love ____ in   vain. ____
But   what - ev - er   road ____ you   choose, ____

____ And   in   my   heart   you'll   al - ways   stay ____
____ And   in   my   heart   you   will ____ re - main ____
____ I'm   right   be - hind   you   win ____ or   lose, ____

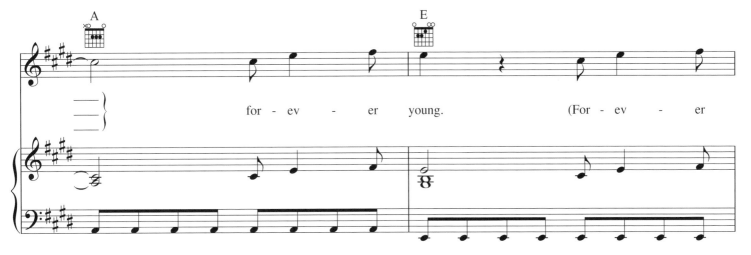

for - ev - er young. (For - ev - er

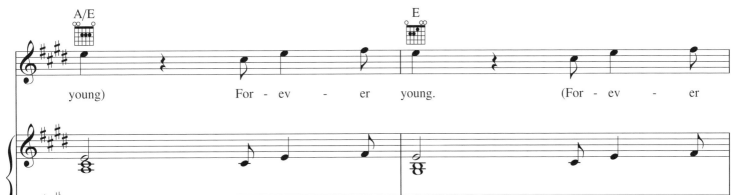

young) For - ev - er young. (For - ev - er

young) ___ May good young) ___

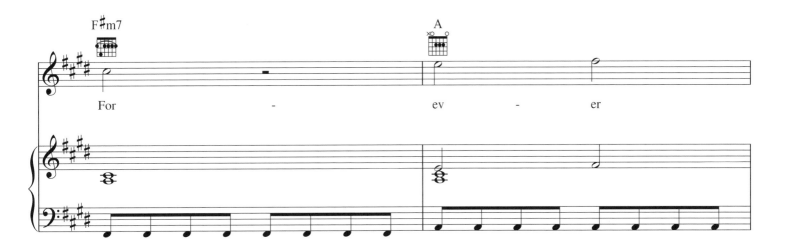

For - ev - er

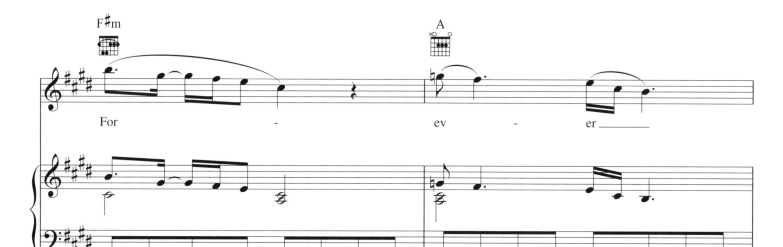

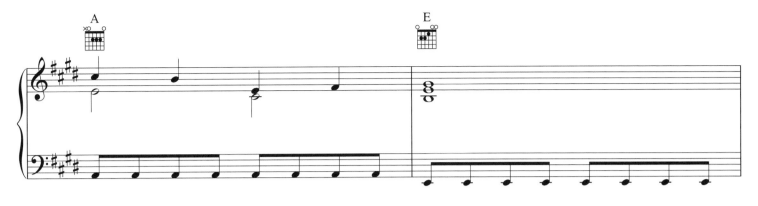

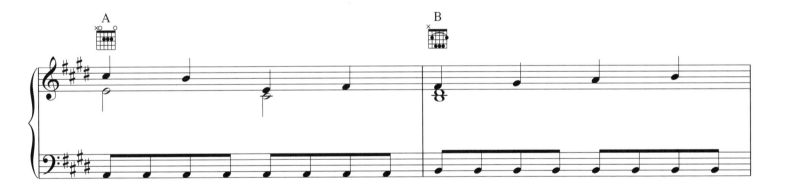

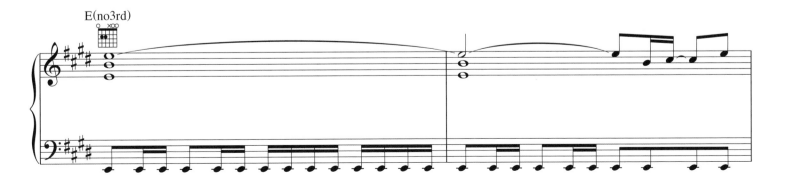

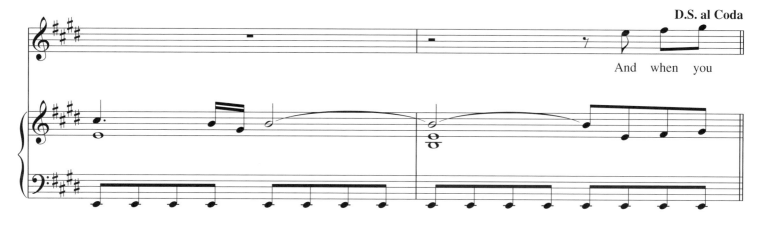

D.S. al Coda

And when you

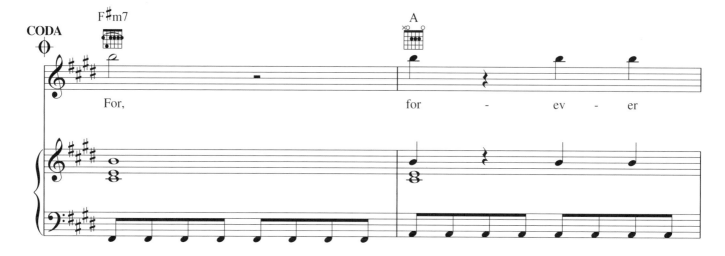

CODA

F#m7

A

For,   for - ev - er

E

young. _____

F#m7   A   E

For -   ev -   er   young. _____

LISTEN TO YOUR HEART

Words and Music by PER GESSLE
and MATS PERSSON

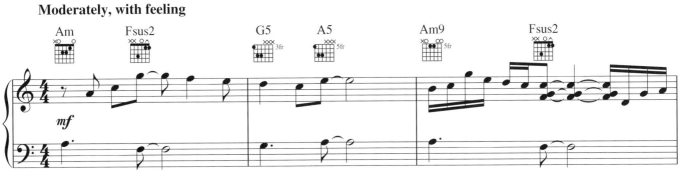

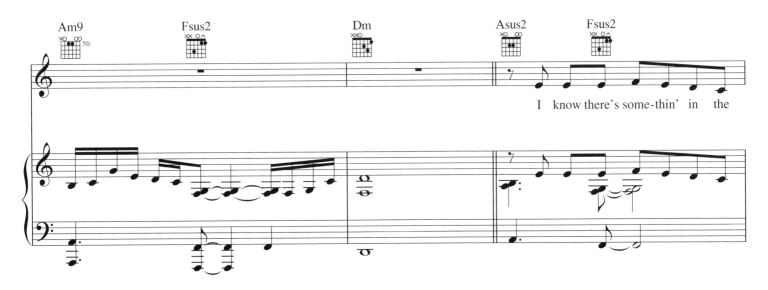

I know there's some-thin' in the

wake of your smile. ___ I get a no - tion from the look in your eyes, ___ yeah.

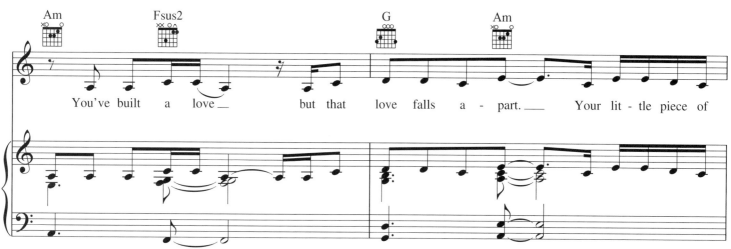

You've built a love ___ but that love falls a-part. ___ Your lit-tle piece of

heav-en turns to dark. ___ Lis-ten to your heart _____ when he's

call-ing for ___ you. _____ Lis-ten to your heart, _____ there's noth-ing

else you can ___ do. _____ I don't know where you're go-ing ___ and ___

To Coda

I don't know why _____ but lis-ten to your heart _____ be-fore _____

_____ you tell _ him _ good - bye. _____

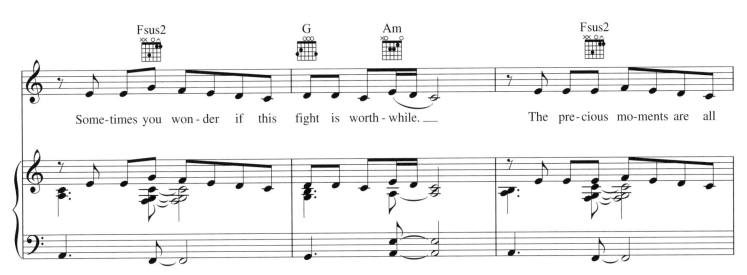

Some-times you won-der if this fight is worth-while. ___ The pre-cious mo-ments are all

lost in the tide, __ yeah. __ They're swept a-way __ and noth-ing is what it seems. __ The feel-ing of be-

D.S. al Coda

long-ing ___ to your dreams. _____ Lis-ten to your

CODA

___ you tell him __ good - bye. _____

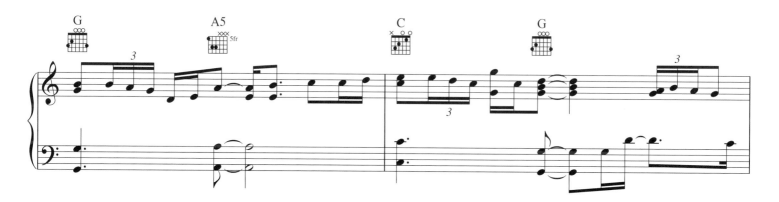

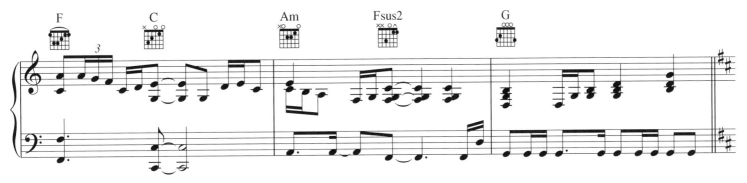

And there are voic - es that want to be heard. _____ So much to men-tion but you

can't find the words. _____ The scent of mag - ic. The beau - ty that's been ____

when love was wild - er ____ than the wind. _____ Lis - ten to your

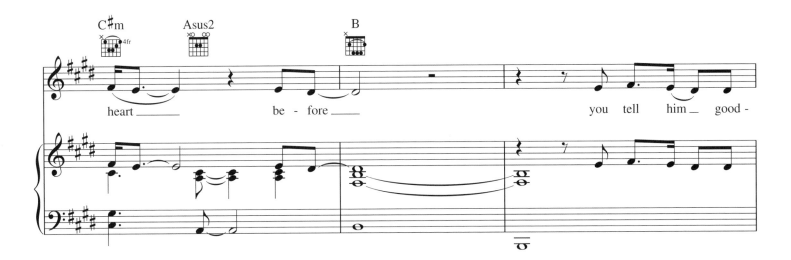

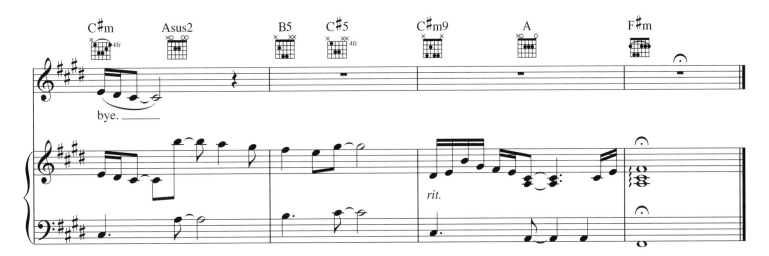

I HOPE YOU DANCE

Words and Music by TIA SILLERS
and MARK D. SANDERS

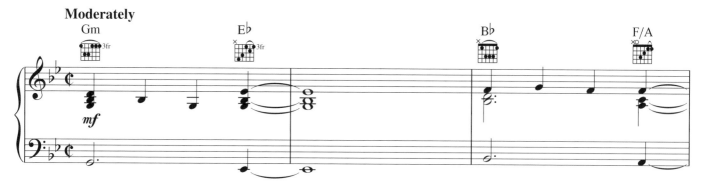

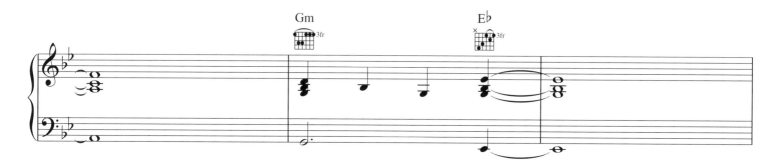

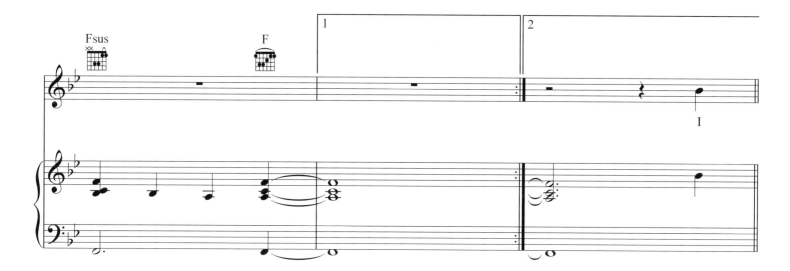

hope you nev - er lose _____ your sense of won - der.
nev - er fear _____ those _____ moun - tains in the dis - tance.

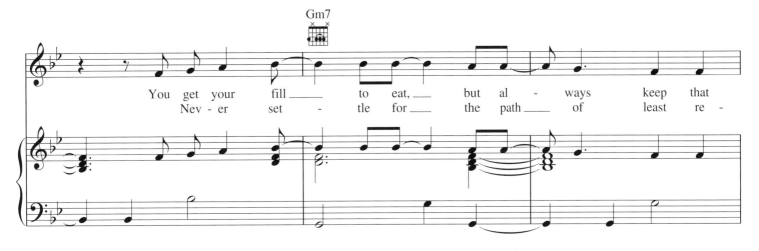

You get your fill ___ to eat, ___ but al - ways keep that
Nev - er set - tle for ___ the path ___ of least re -

hun - ger.   May you nev - er take ___ one
sist - ance.   Liv - in' might mean tak - in'

sin - gle breath ___ for grant - ed.   God for - bid ___
chanc - es if they're worth tak - in'.   Lov - in' might ___

___ love ev - er leave ___ you emp - ty - hand - ed.
___ be a mis - take, ___ but it's ___ worth mak - in'.

I hope you still _____ feel small _____ when you stand be-side _____ the
Don't let _____ some hell - bent _____ heart leave _____ you

o - cean. When-ev - er one _____ door clos - es, I _____
bit - ter. When you come close _____ to sell - in' out, _____

_____ hope one _____ more o - pens. Prom - ise me _____
_____ re - con - sid - er. Give the heav -

_____ that you'll _____ give faith _____ a fight - ing
- ens a - bove more _____ than just a pass - ing

chance.)
glance.)

And when you get the choice to

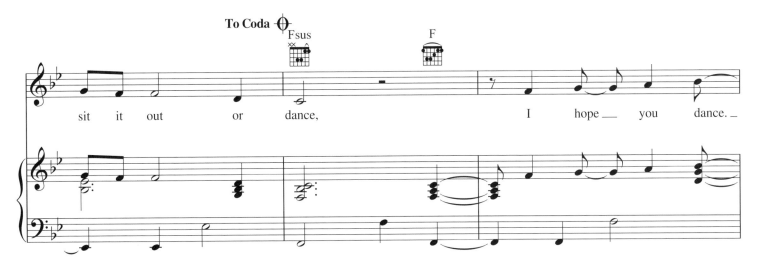

sit it out or dance,

I hope __ you dance. __

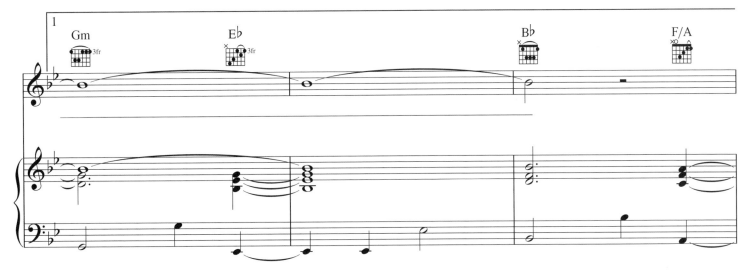

I hope __ you dance. ___

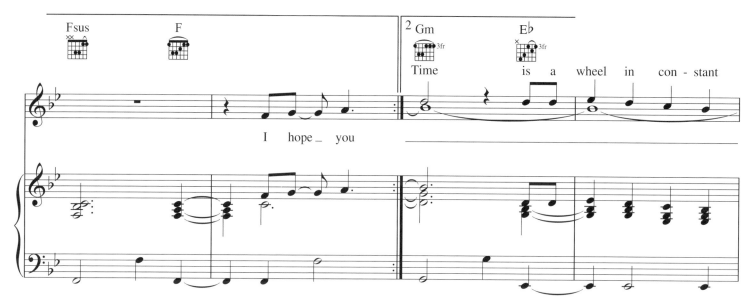

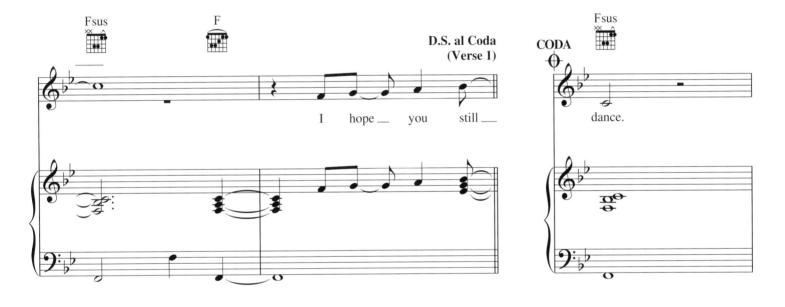

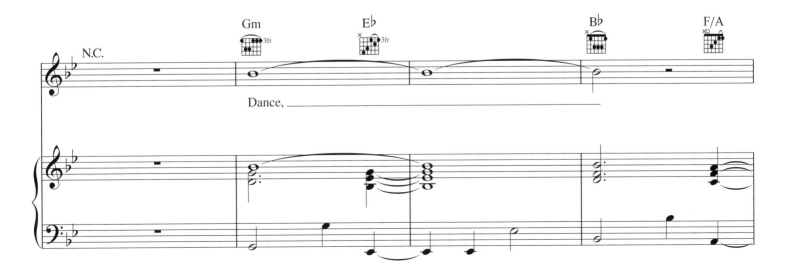

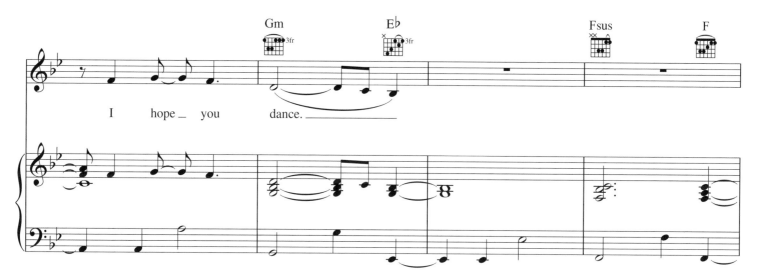

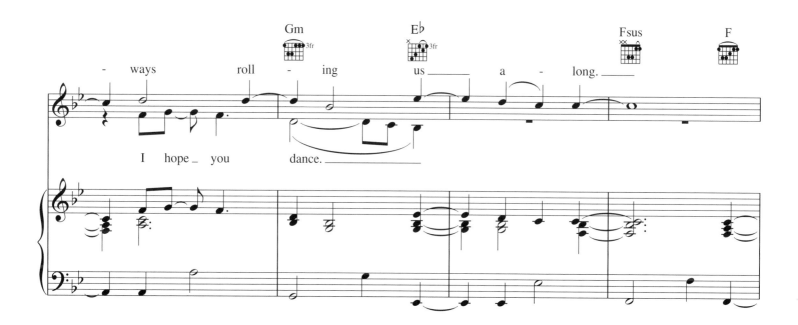

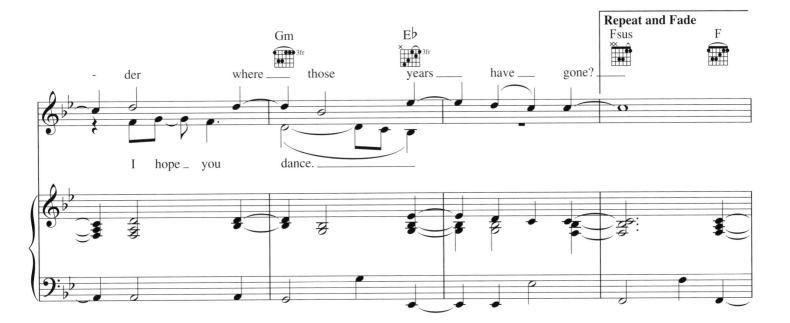

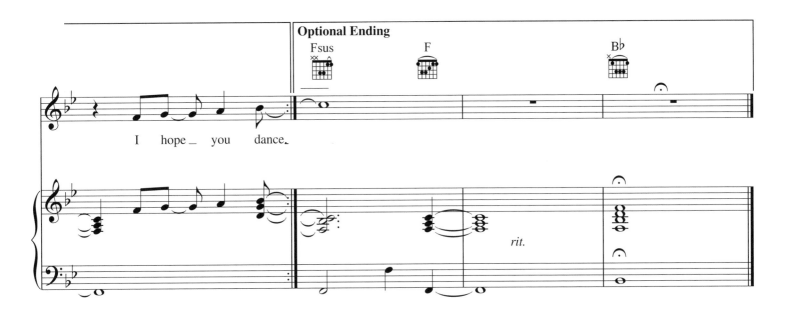

LEAN ON ME

Words and Music by
BILL WITHERS

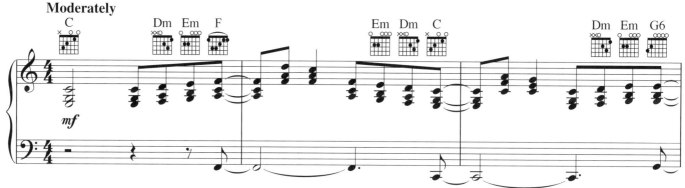

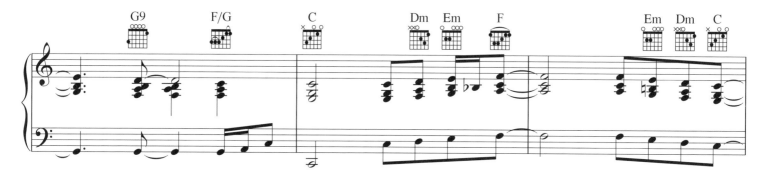

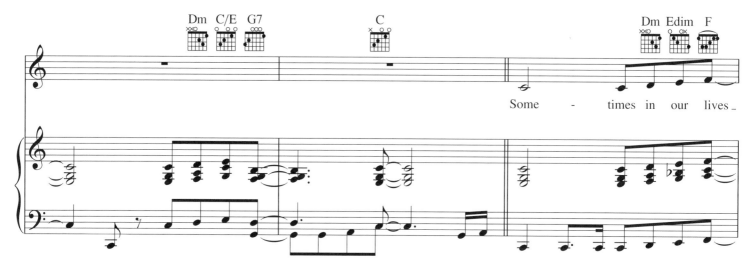

Some - times in our lives _

we all have pain, ___ we all have sor - row, ___

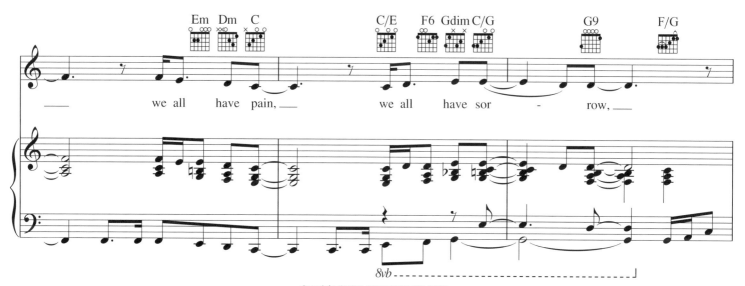

but   if we are wise _____   we know that there's _

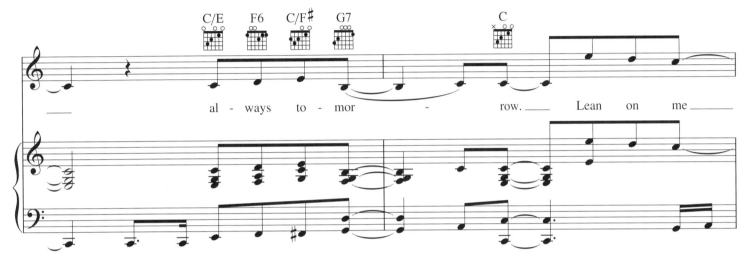

_   al - ways to - mor - row. _____ Lean on me _____

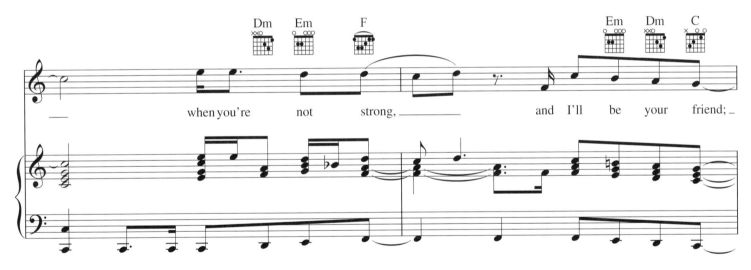

_   when you're not strong, _____ and I'll be your friend; _

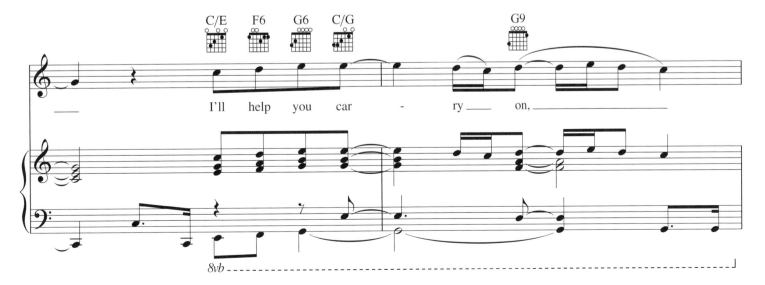

_   I'll help you car - ry ___ on,

8vb -

for no one can fill _____ those of your needs ___

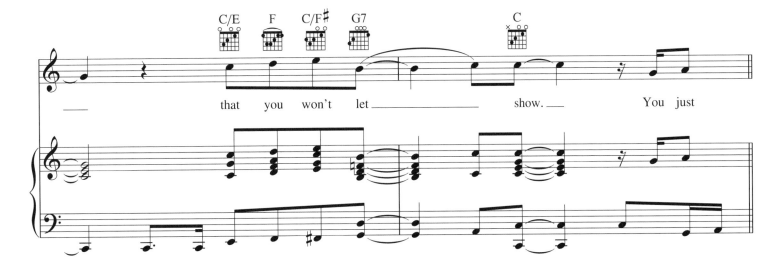

___ that you won't let _____ show. ___ You just

call on me, broth - er, when you need a ___ hand. ___ We all _____

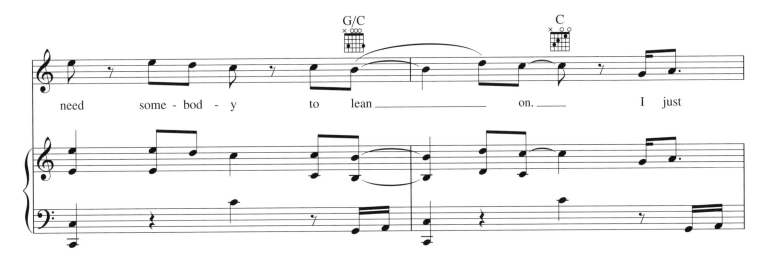

need some - bod - y to lean _____ on. _____ I just

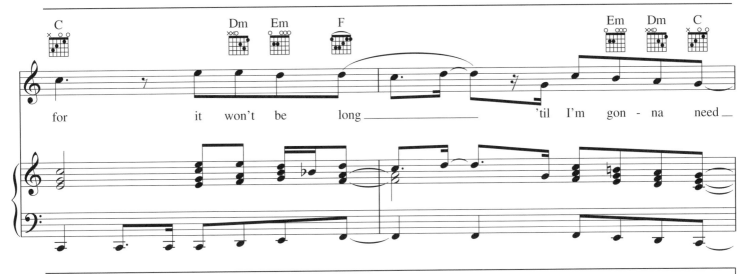

for   it won't be long _____ 'til I'm gon-na need __

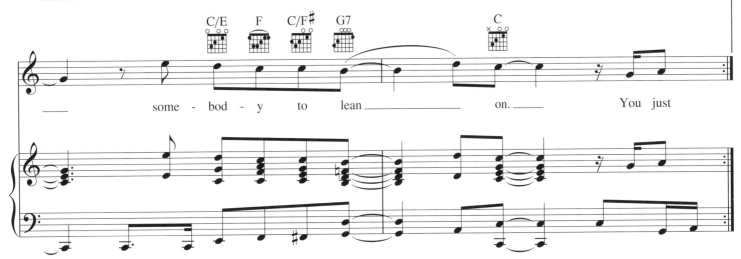

__ some-bod-y to lean _____ on. ___ You just

__ on. ___   If   there is a load ___

you have to bear _____   that you can't

8vb -

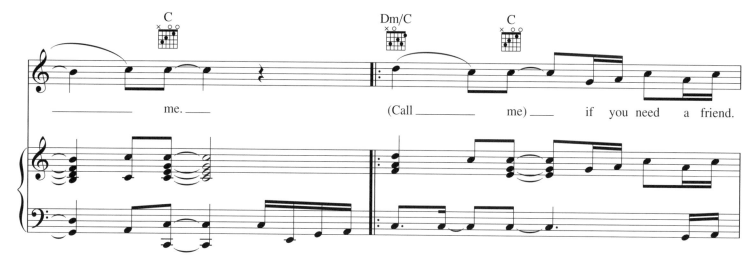

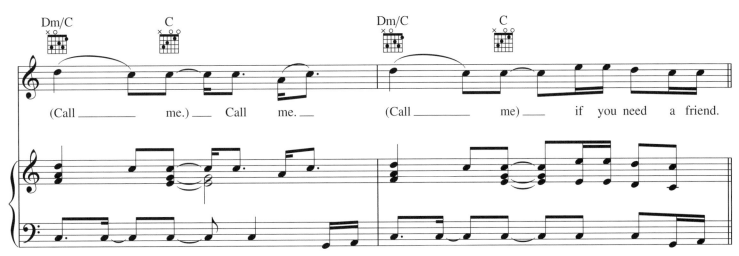

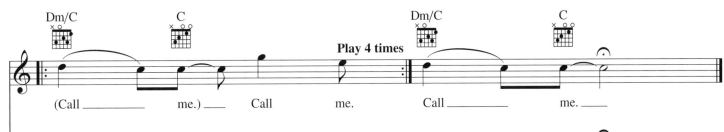

SEASONS OF LOVE

from RENT

Words and Music by
JONATHAN LARSON

love? _____ Meas-ure in love.

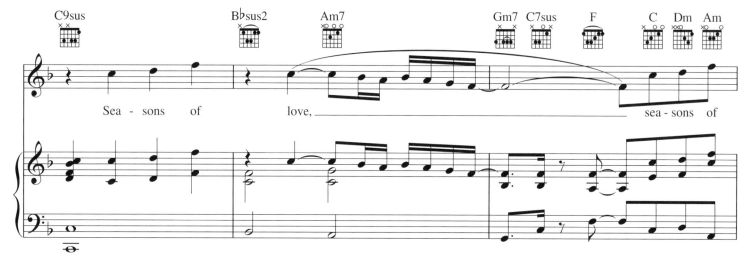

Sea - sons of love, _____ sea - sons of

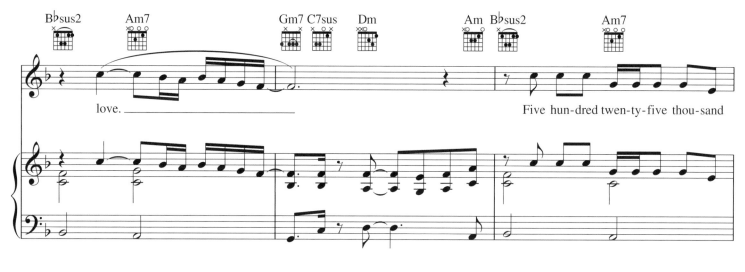

love. _____ Five hun-dred twen-ty-five thou-sand

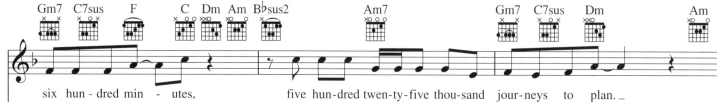

six hun - dred min - utes, five hun-dred twen-ty-five thou-sand jour-neys to plan. _

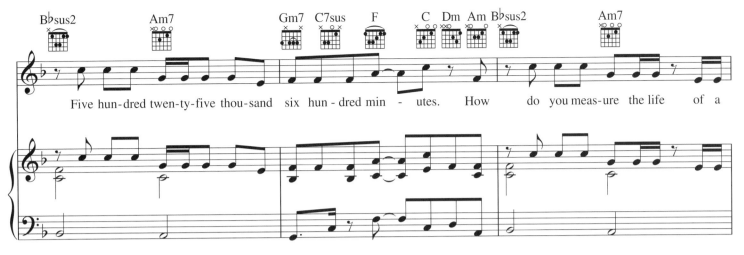

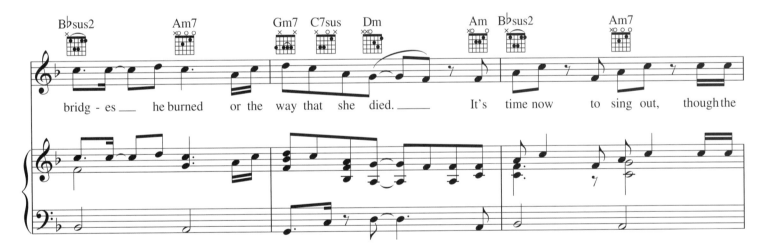

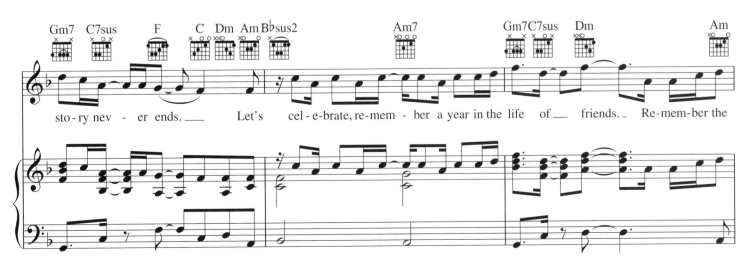

STAND BY ME

Words and Music by JERRY LEIBER,
MIKE STOLLER and BEN E. KING

see,
sea,

oh, I won't
I won't cry,

be a - fraid
I won't cry

no I _____ won't _____
no I _____ won't _____

be a - fraid
shed a tear

just as

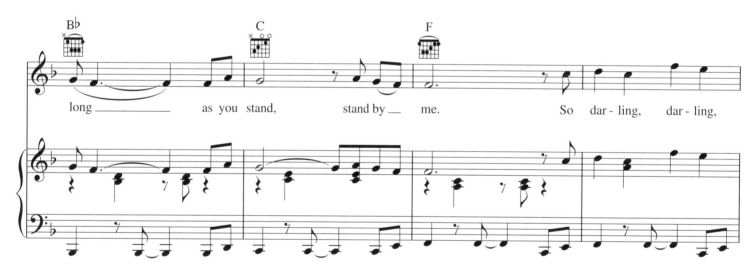

long _____ as you stand,
stand by _ me.
So dar - ling, dar - ling,

stand _____ by me, _____
stand _ by me,
oh

A THOUSAND MILES

Words and Music by
VANESSA CARLTON

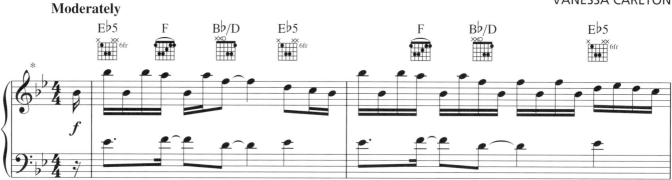

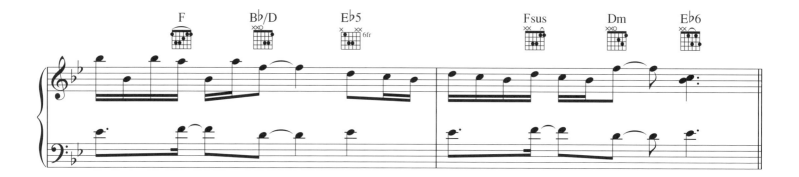

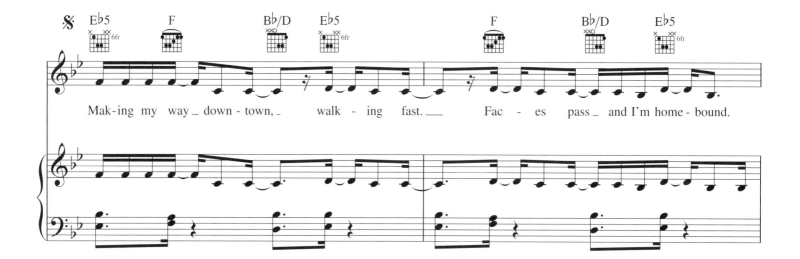

Mak-ing my way_ down-town,_ walk-ing fast._ Fac-es pass_ and I'm home-bound.

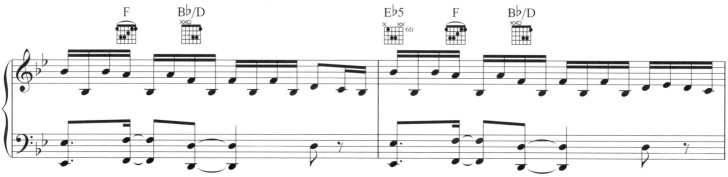

* Recorded a half step higher.

216

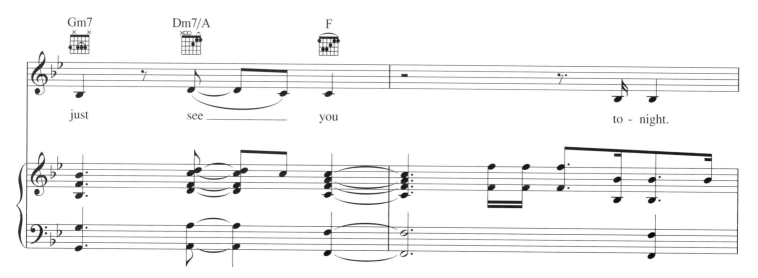

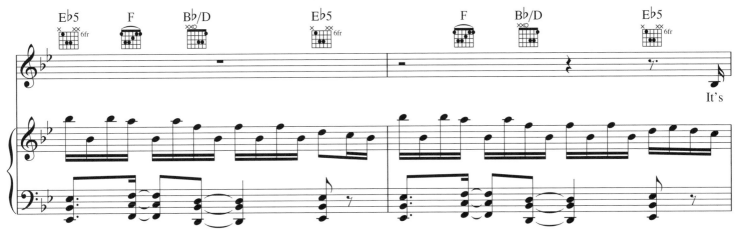

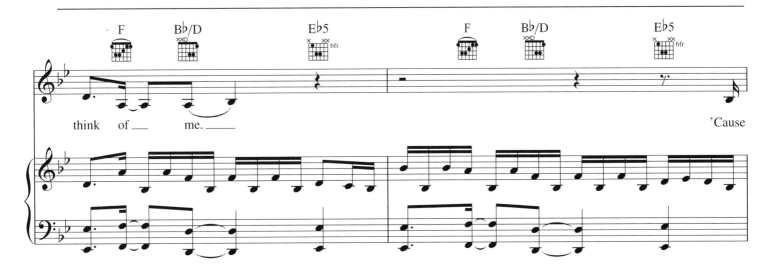

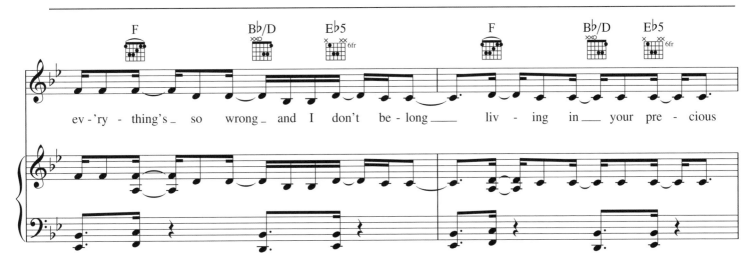

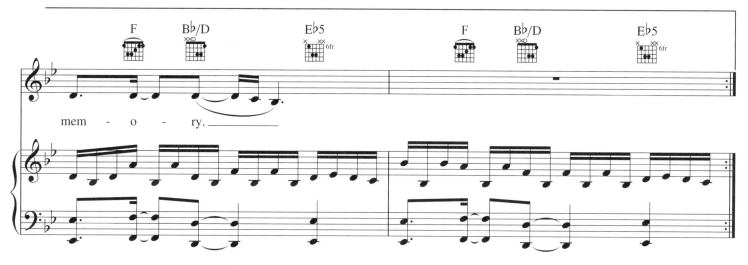

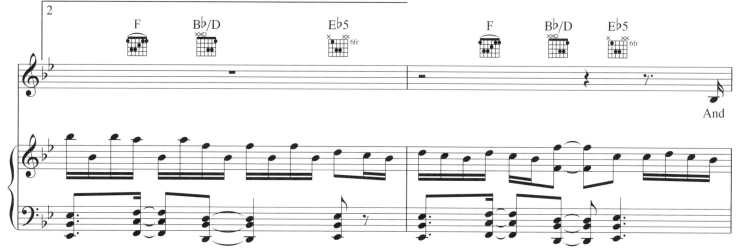

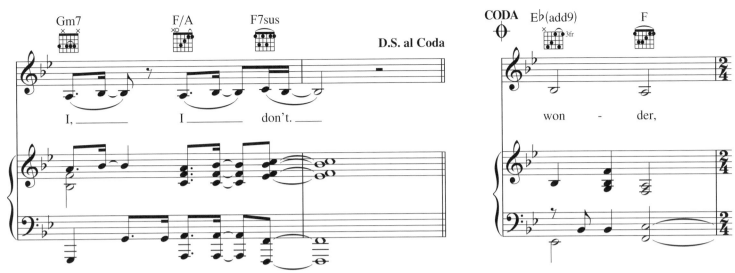

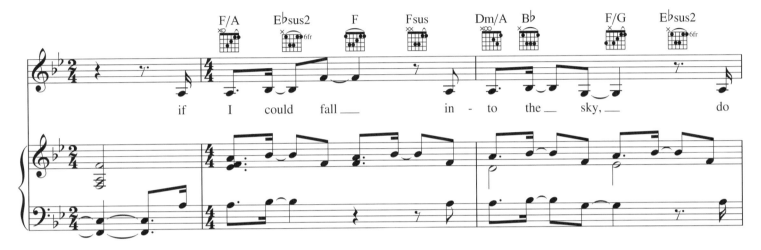

just see _____ you. _____ If

I could _ fall ____ in - to the _ sky, _____ do

you think _ time ____ would pass me _ by? _____ 'Cause

you know _ I'd ____ walk ____ a thou - sand _ miles ____ if I ____ could

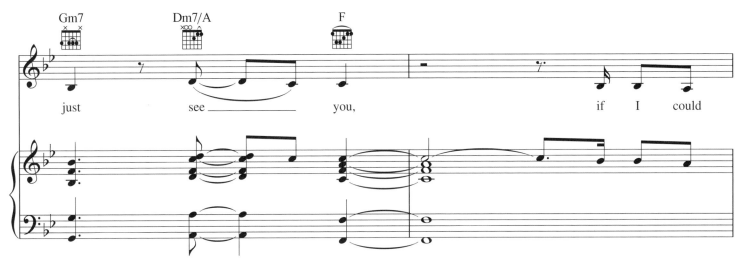

just see _____ you, if I could

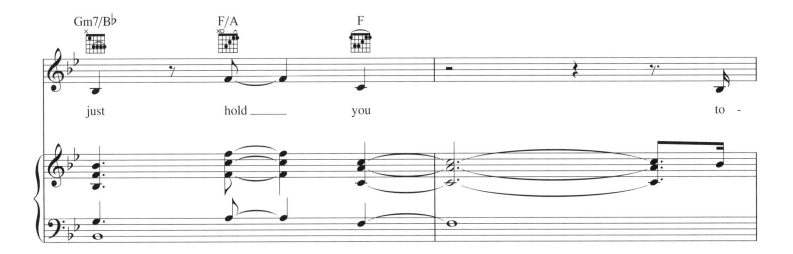

just hold _____ you to -

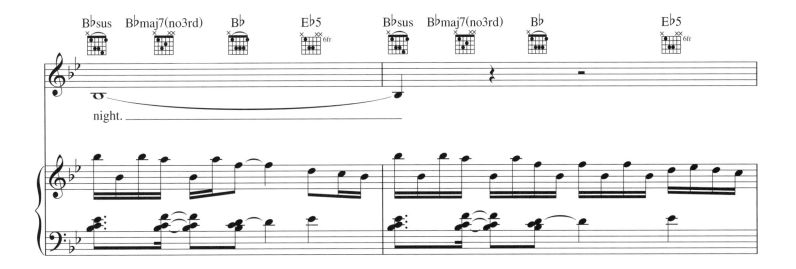

night. _____

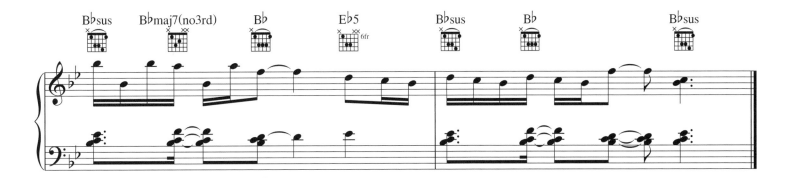

YOU RAISE ME UP

Words and Music by BRENDAN GRAHAM
and ROLF LOVLAND

Moderately slow

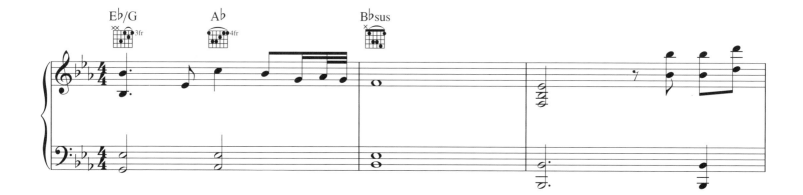

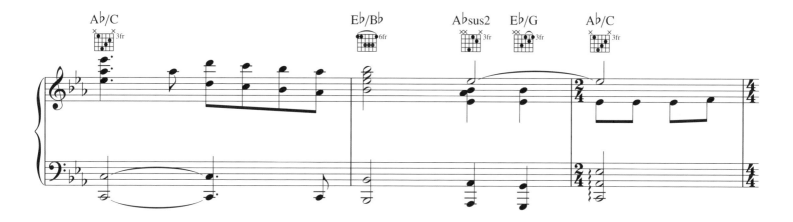

When I am down ___ and oh, my soul's so wea-ry, when trou-bles

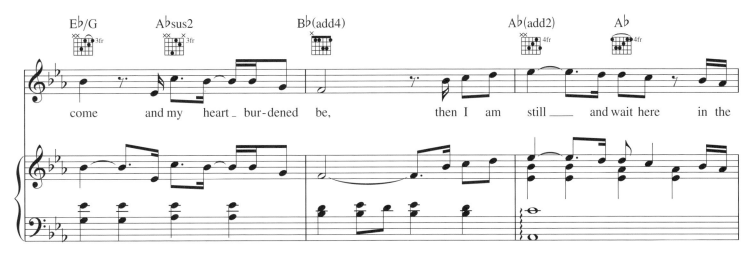

come and my heart ___ bur-dened be, then I am still ___ and wait here in the

si - lence un - til you come and sit a while ___ with me. You raise me

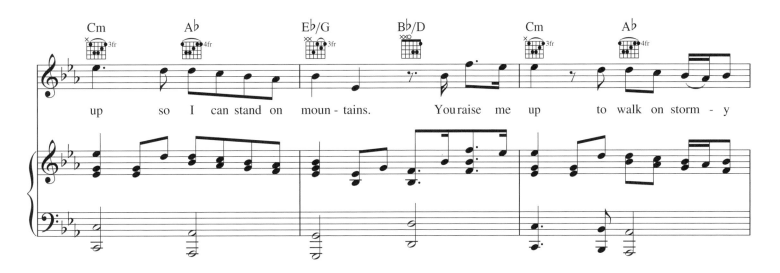

up so I can stand on moun - tains. You raise me up to walk on storm - y

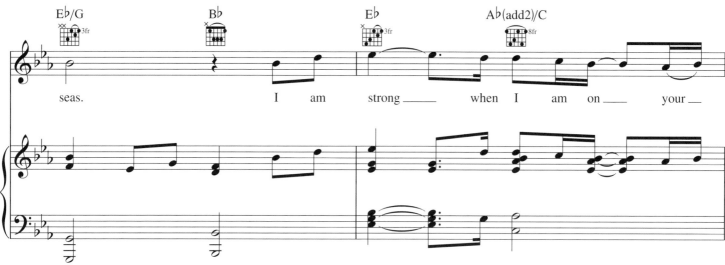

seas.   I am strong _____ when I am on _____ your _____

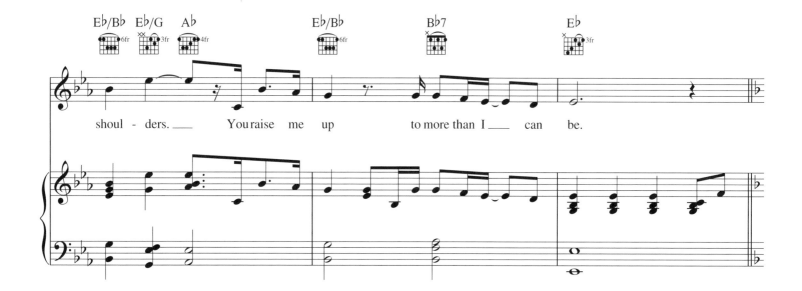

shoul - ders. _____ You raise me up   to more than I _____ can be.

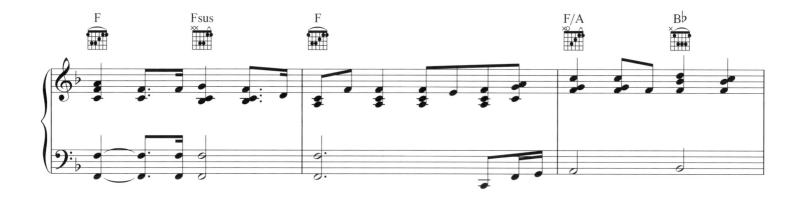

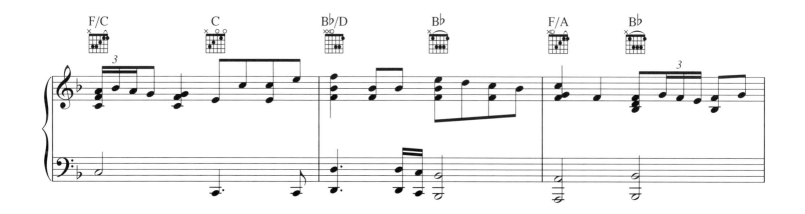

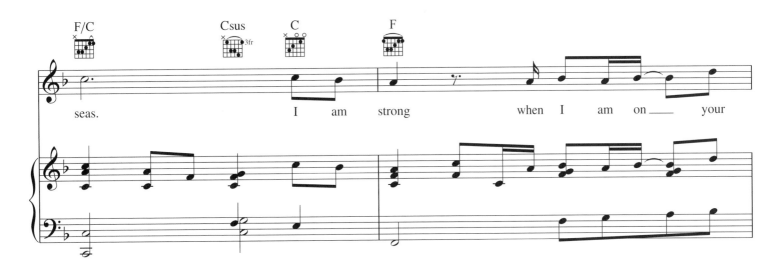

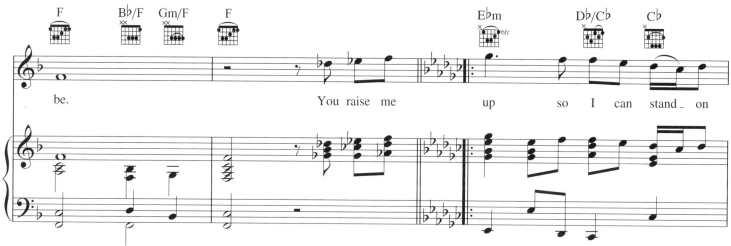

be. You raise me up so I can stand on

moun - tains. You raise me up to walk on storm - y

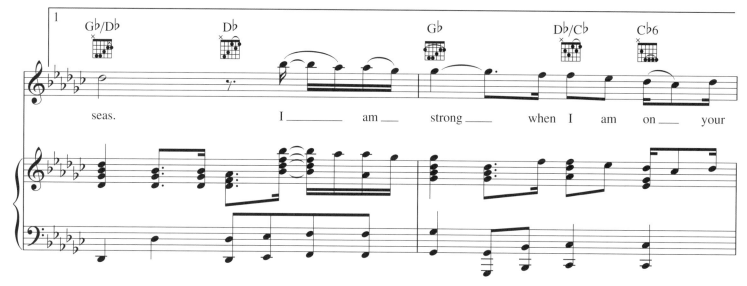

seas. I _____ am _____ strong _____ when I am on _____ your

shoul - ders. You raise me up to more than I _____ can

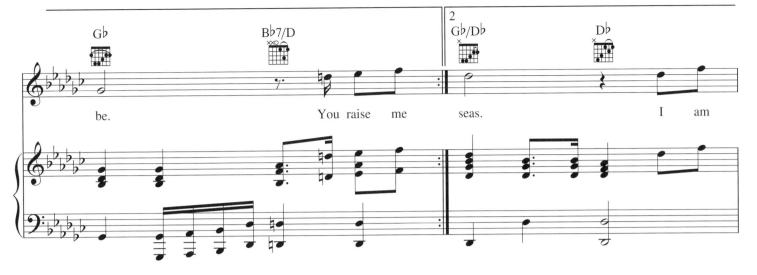

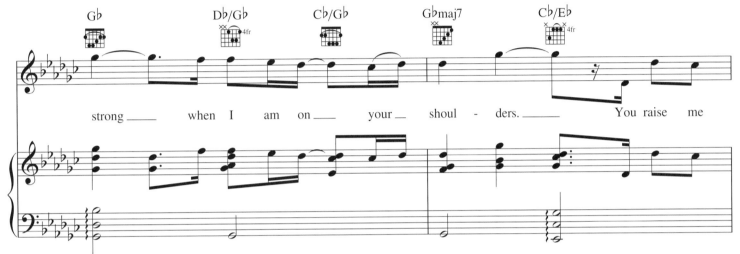

YOU'VE GOT A FRIEND

Words and Music by
CAROLE KING

Moderately

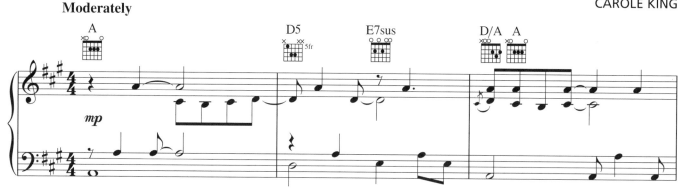

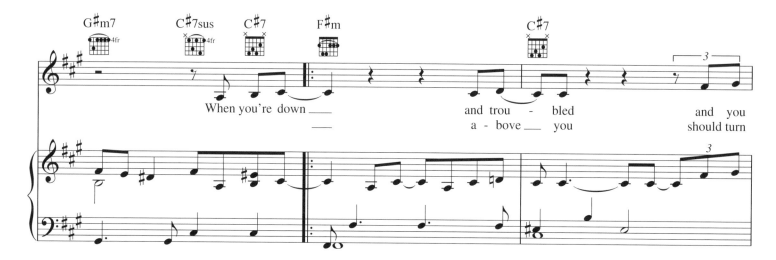

When you're down ___ and trou - bled and you
___ a - bove ___ you should turn

need a help - ing hand ___ and noth - ing, whoa,
dark and full of clouds ___ and that old north

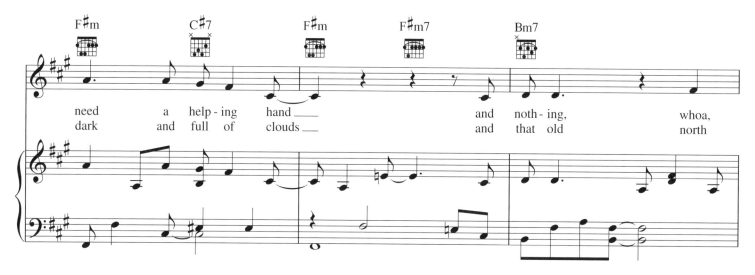

noth - ing is go - ing right, ___
wind should be - gin ___ to blow, ___

close your eyes __ and think of me __ and soon I will __ be there __
keep your head __ to - geth - er and call my name _____ out

__ loud, _____ now; to bright-en up e - ven your dark - est night. __
soon I'll be knock - ing up - on __ your door. __

You just call __ out my name, __

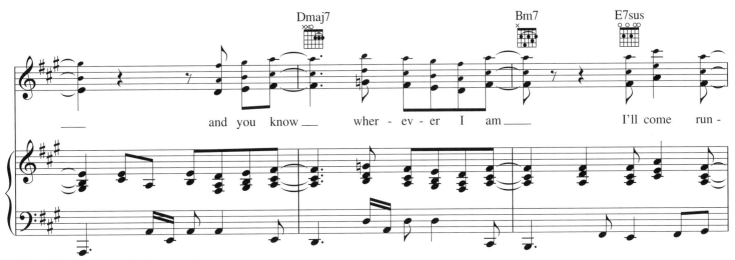

and you know __ wher - ev - er I am __ I'll come run -

Vocal harmony sung 2nd time only

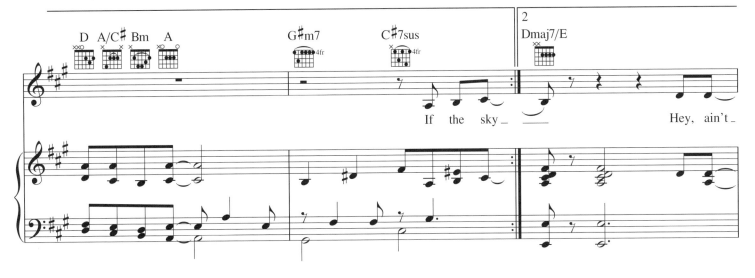

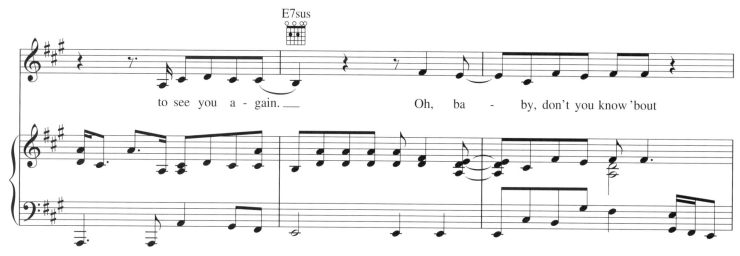

YOU'LL BE IN MY HEART
(Pop Version)
from Walt Disney Pictures' TARZAN™

Words and Music by
PHIL COLLINS

Come stop your cry - ing; _ it will be all right. Just take my hand,

hold it tight. _____ I will pro - tect you from all a - round _ you.

I will be here; don't you _ cry.

For one so small you
Why can't they un - der - stand the

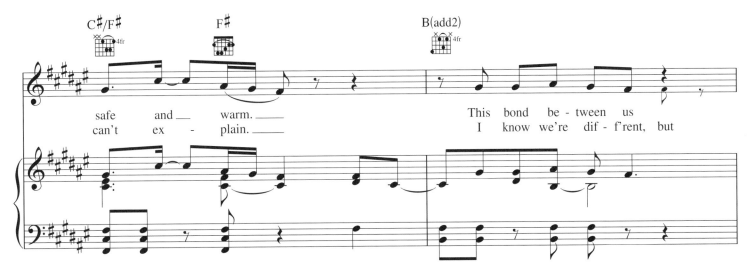

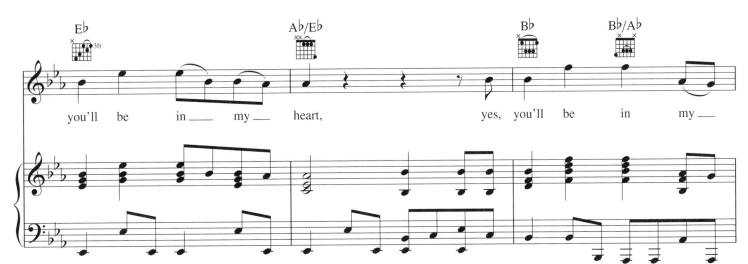

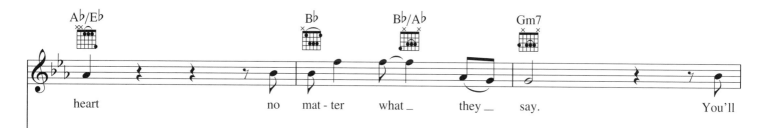

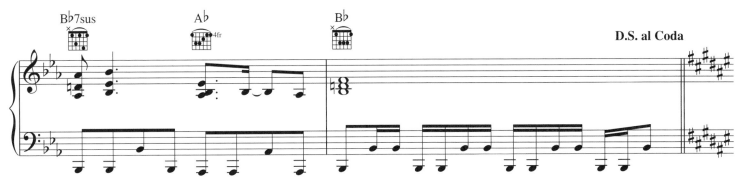

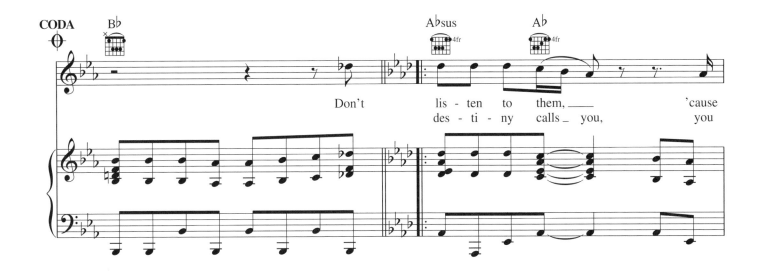

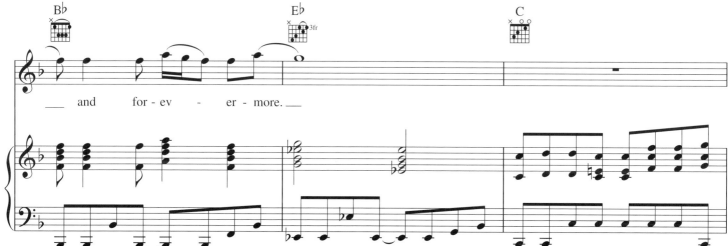

You'll be in _____ my _____ heart
(You'll be here _____ in my heart.) _____
no mat-ter what _____ they _____

say.
(I'll be with you.)
You'll be here in _____ my _____ heart (I'll be there.) al-

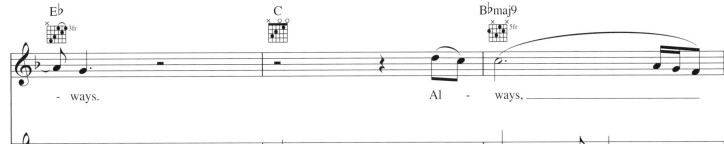

- ways.
Al - ways, _____

I'll be with you.
I'll be

there for ___ you al - ways, al - ways ___ and al - ways. ___

Just look o - ver your shoul - der. Just look o -

- ver your shoul - der. Just look o - ver your shoul - der;

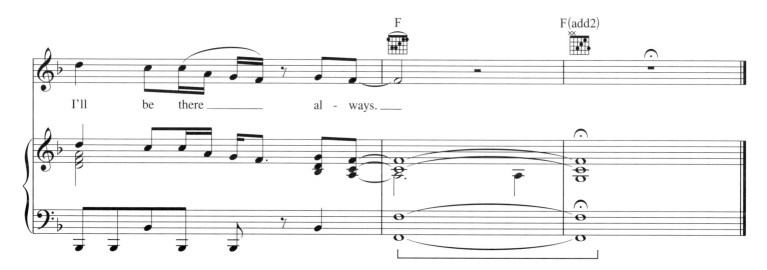

I'll be there ___ al - ways. ___